Leading with Feeling

Leading with Feeling

*Nine Strategies of Emotionally
Intelligent Leadership*

CARY CHERNISS

AND

CORNELIA W. ROCHE

OXFORD
UNIVERSITY PRESS

OXFORD
UNIVERSITY PRESS

Oxford University Press is a department of the University of Oxford. It furthers
the University's objective of excellence in research, scholarship, and education
by publishing worldwide. Oxford is a registered trade mark of Oxford University
Press in the UK and certain other countries.

Published in the United States of America by Oxford University Press
198 Madison Avenue, New York, NY 10016, United States of America.

Library of Congress Cataloging-in-Publication Data
Names: Cherniss, Cary, author. | Roche, Cornelia W., author.
Title: Leading with feeling : nine strategies of emotionally intelligent leadership /
Cary Cherniss and Cornelia W. Roche.
Description: New York : Oxford University Press, 2020. |
Includes bibliographical references and index.
Identifiers: LCCN 2019034042 (print) | LCCN 2019034043 (ebook) |
ISBN 9780190698942 (hardback) | ISBN 9780190698966 (epub) | ISBN 9780190698959
Subjects: LCSH: Leadership. | Communication in management. | Emotional intelligence.
Classification: LCC HD57.7 .C4854 2020 (print) | LCC HD57.7 (ebook) | DDC 658.4/092—dc23
LC record available at https://lccn.loc.gov/2019034042
LC ebook record available at https://lccn.loc.gov/2019034043

9 8 7 6 5 4 3 2 1

Printed by LSC Communications, United States of America

Cary Cherniss: To Deborah, who has been a positive model of emotional intelligence for me and so many others.

Cornelia W. Roche: To Chris, my husband, who has been there through thick and thin. I am forever grateful and happy that we chose to share our life together.

CONTENTS

NINE STRATEGIES OF EMOTIONALLY INTELLIGENT LEADERS

INTRODUCTION

Tom was a young engineer employed at one of the country's largest steel companies.[1] He had been an outstanding individual performer, and now he was a new manager, leading a team responsible for producing steel for a major automobile company. After just a week on the job, Tom and his team met with more than 20 engineers from that other company. As Tom recalled, it was a rude awakening: "I sat in a room with maybe 20 or 25 of their engineers for the annual quality evaluation of suppliers. And I learned for the first time that we were in the bottom of the bottom quartile as a supplier. We had lousy quality, we had lousy invoicing, we had lousy on-time delivery. And this was my first general manager role! I had grown up as an engineer." And how did Tom respond to this unexpected shock?

I had a holy shit moment! I had been in the job literally a week. So part of it was, "Oh my God, what the hell am I going to do?" Also I thought about how my guys had been in the business for a while, and I thought, "What the hell have you been doing?" And I was thinking, "I'm going to clean house!" But then . . . I've learned that you just can't react viscerally every time something comes up because it just scares people away.

So Tom listened attentively as the engineers from the auto company presented their litany of complaints. When they finally finished, he stood up and said, "I wouldn't blame you if you fired us as a supplier. But if you give us a chance to fix these problems, I guarantee you that we will not have this kind of meeting next year."

When Tom met with his team the next morning to discuss the situation, he started by just listening to them. They went on for some time, complaining about how the company and their previous boss had made it impossible for them to provide good products and service. Rather than disagree with them or join in pointing fingers at others, Tom listened. "I didn't think about it at the time," he recalled, "but that first couple of hours was very cathartic for them. My focus was not on beating anyone up but rather, what can we do to fix this?"

The team responded positively to Tom's approach. The next year when they met, representatives of the auto company told Tom that they "never saw any business turn around that quickly in one year." As a result, they began giving Tom's company more business, and Tom went on to a distinguished career, eventually becoming one of his company's top executives.

HOW DID TOM DO IT?

Tom is a good example of how an outstanding leader successfully confronted a daunting challenge. What were the qualities that enabled him to do so? A closer look at what he did reveals that he used emotional intelligence, or "EI." By EI, we mean the ability to accurately identify and understand one's own emotional reactions and those of others. EI also involves the ability to regulate one's emotions, to use them to make good decisions and act effectively.[2]

In Tom's case, the challenge began with the shock of discovering just how badly his work group had done in meeting the needs of a very important customer. He was not only dismayed; he also was not at all sure how to deal with the situation. His stress levels were skyrocketing. Such stress can be incapacitating. Even when we are able to push through it, high levels of stress significantly impede our ability to figure out how to deal with problems such as the one Tom faced.[3] Stress also triggers the "fight-or-flight" response, which was reflected in Tom's initial impulse to react punitively toward his subordinates (to "clean house"). So Tom's first task was to manage his own emotional response.

Once Tom understood what he had to do about his own emotions, his next challenge was to deal effectively with the emotions of the other company's engineers. How did he do so? He remained calm, he listened attentively, and then he *joined with* them. He did not act defensively; he did not argue or disagree or minimize. If anything, he went one better when he said, "If I were you, I wouldn't blame you if you fired us as a supplier." This one simple statement, delivered calmly, conveyed to the other side that Tom had heard them, and he understood how upset they were about the situation. Tom then ended on a positive note. He promised that his group would work on the problems and that within a year their performance would improve significantly.

After the meeting with the auto company's engineers, Tom faced another challenge: managing his own group's emotions. He could tell that they were feeling "beaten up" and that further criticisms and attacks by their new boss would not be an effective way to motivate them to work hard to fix the problems. So he met with them the next day and spent some time just listening to them "vent." Many bosses probably would have seen their team's behavior as whining, refusing to take responsibility, and shifting the blame onto others. But Tom understood that the team needed some time for emotional catharsis, so he listened sympathetically. When they seemed ready to move on, Tom wasted no time in turning the focus to looking for ways to fix the problems.

Tom continued to use his emotional intelligence during the next year, and it paid off. His team went from being at the bottom of the list of suppliers to the very top.

LEARNING HOW OUTSTANDING LEADERS USE THEIR EMOTIONAL INTELLIGENCE

We met Tom as part of a study on how outstanding leaders use emotional intelligence to achieve their goals. We asked executive coaches, management consultants, and other human resource development professionals to identify star leaders who were "effective" and seemed to "use and manage emotions especially well." Our rationale for selecting the leaders in this way was that we wanted a sample of individuals who were likely to use emotional intelligence in many situations.

Altogether, we interviewed 25 mid-level and senior-level leaders from different kinds of organizations, including large corporations, smaller family-owned businesses, and private nonprofit social service agencies. The leaders also came from public human service agencies, health care organizations, and educational settings ranging from nursery schools to a university. There were 12 men and 13 women. (For a list of the leaders and the kinds of organizations in which they worked, see Appendix A; for more details on the research, see Appendix B.)

If we had given these leaders a test to determine how emotionally intelligent they were, they probably would have scored high. But we believed it would be more interesting and useful to learn *how* the leaders *used* their emotional intelligence to deal with challenging situations. Although it is possible, with concerted effort, to increase our emotional intelligence over time, *it is usually easier for us to learn how to use the EI we already have.* So we asked the leaders to describe some incidents in which they had "managed or used emotion . . . to deal with a problem or achieve a goal." The leaders talked about 126 such situations. We recorded and transcribed the interviews, and after studying them closely, some intriguing themes began to emerge. These themes pointed to nine *strategies* that can help leaders or potential leaders to be more successful—both at work and in their personal lives.

In this book, we present those strategies, along with many examples demonstrating how the leaders used them in actual situations. We believe that these lessons and case examples can help anyone in a leadership position to use their emotional intelligence more strategically and effectively.

WHAT IS EMOTIONAL INTELLIGENCE?

For most of the past century, psychologists assumed that there was just one kind of intelligence and that it made a big difference when it came to performance in all but the simplest of jobs. That intelligence was *cognitive* intelligence, the foundation for basic mental functions such as memory, reasoning, and analytical thinking. But then, in 1983, Harvard psychologist Howard Gardner wrote a paradigm-breaking book in which he argued that there were *multiple* intelligences. In addition to separate "linguistic" and "logical-mathematical" intelligences, there was visual-spatial intelligence and musical intelligence. Great athletes excelled in bodily kinesthetic intelligence. Then there were the intrapersonal and interpersonal intelligences. Gardner argued that these intelligences were distinct; people can excel at one type but not others. He also proposed that linguistic and logical-mathematical intelligences, which are the ones measured by IQ tests and related instruments, are not the only kind of intelligence that is important for success and happiness in life.[4]

The door was open: The idea that there was more than one intelligence became widely accepted. Other psychologists began to propose other types of intelligence.[5] Then, in 1990, Peter Salovey of Yale University and Jack Mayer of the University of New Hampshire published a paper in a scientific journal in which they proposed that there was an "emotional intelligence."[6] Their idea was picked up by Daniel Goleman, a psychologist and science writer at the *New York Times*, who wrote a book about it.[7] When that book appeared in 1995, it quickly jumped onto the bestseller list and remained there for a year-and-a-half. Eventually it was translated into more than 40 languages.

Although there are now several different models of emotional intelligence, they all begin with the idea that EI involves the abilities to recognize and regulate emotions in oneself and others.[8] The models also propose that there are several different aspects to EI. It is not just the ability to stay calm in a crisis, though that is part of it. Nor is it merely the ability to tune in to how others are feeling, or figure out why they are feeling the way they do. One can be strong in one aspect of EI but not others. Too often, in fact, leaders are very good at managing their own emotions in difficult situations but less effective in sensing how others are feeling or in crafting effective approaches to help them manage those feelings. Conversely, there are leaders who are very aware of their own emotional reactions and those of others, but they are not able to manage those emotions in ways that help people to move ahead in dealing with difficult situations. And then there are those who excel in most, if not all, of the dimensions. Those were the ones we wanted to study.

THE IMPACT OF EMOTIONAL INTELLIGENCE
ON LEADER EFFECTIVENESS

When we ask groups of people to think about a very effective leader and then identify the qualities that make him or her so effective, they often come up with qualities such as "empathic," "inspiring," "decisive," "trustworthy," "calm," and having "good judgment." What all of these qualities have in common is that they seem to involve emotional intelligence.

The history of many of the most enduringly successful high-tech companies demonstrates how superior cognitive intelligence by itself is often not enough in the long run for effective leadership. Take Google as an example. Google was founded by Larry Page and Sergey Brin, two young people who were immersed in the technology that Google developed. As the company grew and matured, they hired an outsider, Eric Schmidt, to come in and take charge. According to one report, "A key part of Mr. Schmidt's role was as peacemaker. This meant softening the founders' sometimes harsh feedback to employees, carrying out their wishes and smoothing over differences when they arose, all while managing the competing demands and interests of the executives reporting to him." Schmidt thrived in the role because he reportedly was "very good at bringing people together, getting people to agree."[9]

Tech companies are not the only kind of organization that needs emotionally intelligent leaders. The same appears to be true for a very different kind of organization: the military. In a story on how the role of a senior military leader has changed in recent years, Thom Shanker wrote, "Mastery of battlefield tactics and a knack for leadership are only prerequisites. Generals and other top officers are now expected to be city managers, cultural ambassadors, public relations whizzes and politicians as they deal with multiple missions and constituencies in the war zone, in allied capitals—and at home."[10]

In addition to many compelling anecdotes, there now is a growing body of empirical evidence suggesting a clear link between emotional intelligence and leadership effectiveness. For example, in one study the bosses, peers, and subordinates of top-level executives in a large financial services firm rated the executives' EI.[11] The researchers then looked at the executives' performance and potential ratings over a 3-year period. They found that the most successful executives were rated higher in competencies such as Self-Confidence, Achievement Motivation, and Organizational Awareness. They also scored especially high on Inspirational Leadership and Change Catalyst.[12]

Another study looked at a very different group of leaders—supervisors in a large manufacturing organization. The researchers assessed the leaders' EI with a test that, like a traditional IQ test, required the participants to complete a number of tasks designed to measure different EI abilities. For example, in one subtest the subject had to determine what emotions a person was feeling based on a picture of the person's face. The researchers then asked the supervisors' immediate subordinates to rate their bosses on a measure of managerial effectiveness. The results of the study again indicated a link between EI and performance. The supervisors who were rated highest in effectiveness also scored highest on the EI test.[13]

Several other studies, involving different kinds of leaders working in different kinds of organizations, have produced similar results. They include division presidents in a large, multinational food and beverage company,[14] managers working in a large public service company,[15] and soldiers.[16] In these studies, emotional intelligence predicted performance outcomes such as salary bonuses, performance targets, and ratings by bosses. Other studies have found that a leader's EI also has a powerful effect on employees' job satisfaction[17] and their emotional commitment.[18]

A leader's EI also seems to have an impact on the physical and mental health of an organization's employees. A wide-ranging review of nearly 30 years of research found that leader behaviors and leadership styles closely associated with EI were linked with less stress and greater physical well-being in followers.[19] For instance, in one study, 60 IT employees working in a large medical facility reported on whether they were experiencing physical symptoms such as headaches, high blood pressure, and stomachaches daily for 2 weeks. Meanwhile, their supervisors completed a widely used measure of empathy. The results showed that groups of employees with empathic managers experienced lower levels of somatic complaints.[20]

BUSINESS LEADERS NOW RECOGNIZE THE IMPORTANCE OF EMOTIONAL INTELLIGENCE

Given the growing evidence for the importance of emotional intelligence, it is not surprising that business schools increasingly emphasize it in their curriculum. For instance, in 2011 the new dean of the Harvard Business School, Nitin Nohria, decided that "there were three issues in particular that we need to focus more on in our curriculum." The first one he mentioned was "leadership, in particular to develop emotional intelligence." The other two were globalization and developing in students an "entrepreneurial imagination."[21]

As Kevin Engholm, a managing director and head of institutional learning and development at Citi noted: "As the pace of change in organizations continues to accelerate and many fear that jobs will be replaced by machines (estimates are as high as 47% of all jobs in the U.S. will be vulnerable in the future), leaders/managers are going to increasingly need to express empathy and help people navigate uncertainty and adapt to change. Similarly, as work becomes increasingly automated, the deeply human characteristics that are embodied in EI become even more important."[22] He went on to observe that EI will also become more important "in work across large organizations with individuals in different geographies and with different cultural backgrounds."

WHY EMOTIONAL INTELLIGENCE IS IMPORTANT FOR EFFECTIVE LEADERSHIP

One reason that EI helps leaders to be more effective is because it enhances their ability to influence others.[23] Organizational leaders have many ways of influencing others.[24] Some people will obey their leaders simply because the leaders have the formal authority to lead. They do what the boss wants because the boss is the boss. Leaders also can influence others through their control of rewards and punishments. And a leader can exert even more influence over others if they perceive the leader as having more relevant knowledge or expertise about an issue than anyone else in their group. However, leaders increasingly must rely on how they are viewed by others. People are more likely to comply with requests that come from someone they admire, respect, and trust.[25]

Gaining the trust of others requires emotional intelligence. As George S. Barrett, the chairman and CEO of Cardinal Health, said in an interview, trust has to do with being clear about what you believe: "People have to trust that you have a point of view about what this enterprise is going to look like."[26] This clarity requires the *courage* of one's convictions, and courage is ultimately about being able to manage one's anxiety in the face of risk or adversity.

Barrett also thought that trust comes from being able to understand one's followers: "People . . . have to trust that you understand them, that you get them, and that you have their interests at heart." Thus, gaining the trust of others also requires the ability to perceive accurately how others are feeling and why they feel that way.[27]

Charisma also helps leaders influence others, and emotional intelligence appears to play a central role here as well. As one researcher noted, "The ability of charismatic leaders to identify, empathize with, and model emotions and emotional behavior is critical to their success, and they gain legitimacy by modeling emotions for their followers."[28] Charismatic leaders seem to excel in the ability to "express emotions and emotional messages,"[29] which often involves the "creative use of words that paint a compelling vision of the future for the organization or work group."[30]

Although influencing others is a critical aspect of leadership, organizational leaders also need to provide a positive climate for their workers in order to sustain high levels of motivation and engagement. Google discovered just how important leaders are for employee engagement when it did extensive research on its own workforce to determine how to best retain the most valued workers. The company formed a research team to look at the reasons why some good workers left, and it found that the most important reason was their boss. When it looked more closely to see what qualities of the boss were most critical, it found that the boss's emotional and social competence was more important than either cognitive intelligence or technical skill. In fact, technical skill ranked last in a list of eight factors. According to Bryant, a journalist who reported on the research, "What employees valued most were even-keeled bosses who made time for one-on-one meetings, who helped people puzzle through problems by asking questions, not dictating answers, and who took an interest in employees' lives and careers."[31]

Google's experience is not unique. Surveys have repeatedly found that bad bosses are usually the number one cause for employees to leave their jobs.[32] And it is often the lack of emotional intelligence in a boss that drives workers to depart.

We often think of effective leaders as possessing two very different sets of qualities. On the one hand, they are strong, firm, and focused. On the other, they also seem to be empathic, caring, and compassionate.[33] Although emotional intelligence would seem to be more important for the softer side of leadership, it also is critical for strong leadership because emotions such as fear of failure and worry about others' opinions can make it difficult for leaders to act decisively.[34] Emotional intelligence is thus vital for being both a strong and a caring leader.[35]

IS EMOTIONAL INTELLIGENCE ALWAYS HELPFUL
FOR LEADERS?

Emotional intelligence is not the only factor that influences a leader's effectiveness; a leader's cognitive abilities, such as memory, reasoning, and attention, also are important.[36] And a leader's values also play a role. At a recent meeting of the Consortium for Research on Emotional Intelligence in Organizations (CREIO), the liveliest topic of discussion was whether leaders with high EI always act ethically and humanely. Stéphane Côté, one of the leading researchers in the field, argued that leaders can, and sometimes do, use EI to manipulate people for their own selfish purposes. The difference between a skillful sociopath and an inspiring moral leader lies not in their EI but in their basic human values. It is thus possible for one to possess a high level of EI but lack basic decency, and those are the most dangerous and destructive leaders.[37]

But what about the leaders who seem to be successful but lack emotional intelligence? If there is a positive link between emotional intelligence and leadership effectiveness, how do we explain them? There are several possible reasons. First, such leaders may achieve short-term success but prove to be ineffective in the long run. A classic example are the "turn-around artists" in the corporate world who cut costs through massive layoffs. The company's stock often goes up as a result, which makes the leader appear successful. However, those layoffs, especially if implemented in a callous way, often do lasting damage that eventually shows up in lost revenue, reduced market share, and lower customer satisfaction. Successful leaders are not necessarily effective leaders.[38]

There are several other reasons why a leader who seems to be lacking in emotional intelligence might appear to be successful. Sometimes, emotionally challenged leaders might succeed due to especially favorable external factors, such as a booming economy or lack of significant competition. It also is possible that the leader is not in a real leadership role, such as the head of a large conglomerate who spends most of his time buying and selling other companies while others are the true leaders running the company. Even if the individual is in a real leadership role, there may be others with high levels of EI who are able to compensate for the formal leader's deficiencies. One other possibility is that the leader's reputation for being deficient in EI is based on anecdotes reflecting a limited and incomplete view of the leader's actual behavior.

HOW DO OUTSTANDING LEADERS *USE* THEIR EMOTIONAL INTELLIGENCE?

Given that emotional intelligence is so important for outstanding leadership, how do great leaders actually *use* their EI to deal effectively with the critical challenges that every leader faces? Knowing that outstanding leaders score high in tests of emotional intelligence is useful, but it does not tell us much about how these leaders actually use those competencies to achieve their goals.[39] A test score does not indicate the specific *strategies* that the leaders use to leverage their EI in challenging situations. Knowing about those strategies would be especially useful for leaders or potential leaders who would like to use the emotional intelligence they already have in order to be more effective.

Our research helped to fill this need. When we asked a sample of outstanding leaders to describe critical incidents in which they had to use or manage emotion, we discovered the strategies that they used. Each incident was unique, and the leaders approached them in a variety of ways. However, when we examined more closely how the leaders went about handling these incidents, we discovered nine common strategies linked to EI abilities and competencies as presented in Box 1.1.

The order of the strategies is based on a prevalent view of how the basic EI abilities relate to each other, which is to see perception and awareness of emotion as the foundation, with understanding and management of emotion building on that foundation. Thus, the first strategy, *monitor the emotional climate*, is linked to perception of emotion. The next set of strategies (e.g., *consider how your own behavior influences others' emotions*) are linked most closely to emotion understanding, and the last

---

Box 1.1   NINE STRATEGIES LINKED TO EMOTIONAL INTELLIGENCE ABILITIES AND COMPETENCIES

1. Monitor the emotional climate.
2. Express your feelings to motivate others.
3. Consider how your own behavior influences others' emotions.
4. Put yourself in others' shoes.
5. Decipher the underlying emotional dynamics of the situation.
6. Reframe how you think about the situation.
7. Create optimal interpersonal boundaries.
8. Seek out others for help in managing emotions.
9. Help others develop their emotional intelligence abilities.

---

group are linked to emotion management. (In Appendix C we show how each strategy is linked to one or more of the EI abilities.)

WHAT COMES NEXT?

In the next nine chapters, we elaborate on each of these strategies and illustrate with many examples how the leaders in our study used them to deal with different circumstances. Each chapter ends with one or more activities designed to help readers apply the strategies and begin developing their skill in doing so. Then, in Chapter 10, we show how the leaders skillfully combined different strategies in order to maximize their impact. Chapter 11 switches the focus from the individual leader to the larger social and organizational context. The chapter identifies the different aspects of an organization that influence how much of their emotional intelligence leaders will use, such as the organization's norms and values and the way in which jobs are designed. It then describes how some organizations have used these aspects to create a more "EI-friendly" environment. The final chapter provides a few guiding principles for using the strategies and concludes by suggesting what leaders can do if they find themselves in an organization that does not support emotionally intelligent behavior.

NOTES

1. The names of all the leaders are pseudonyms, and they are listed in Appendix A. In some cases, we also have made minor changes in the descriptions to maintain the confidentiality of these individuals and their organizations.
2. Mayer, Salovey, and Caruso (2000).
3. Fiedler (2002).
4. There were earlier attempts to identify "non-cognitive" intelligences. One of the earliest was Thorndike's (1920) article, published in *Harper's Magazine*, in which he proposed that there is a "social intelligence." However, Gardner's work is usually considered the beginning of current interest in the topic among psychologists.
5. See, for example, Sternberg's "practical intelligence" (Sternberg, 1985).
6. Salovey and Mayer (1990). Bar-On (1988) had previously developed a measure of "psychological well-being," which he called the "EQ-I," for his unpublished doctoral dissertation. But Salovey and Mayer were the first to use the term *emotional intelligence* in a paper published in a scientific journal.
7. Goleman (1995).
8. One type of model views EI as a limited number of abilities, such as the abilities to perceive and express emotions, to use emotions to facilitate thought, to understand the causes and effects of emotions, and to manage emotions (Mayer, Salovey, & Caruso, 2000; Palmer, Stough, Hamer, & Gignac, 2009). The other type of model includes a number of more specific traits or emotional and social competencies (ESCs) that are important for positive adaptation, such as self-awareness, resilience, empathy, and the ability to influence others (Bar-On, 2000; Goleman, 1998; Petrides & Furnham, 2001).
9. Miller (2011, p. B4).
10. Shanker (2010, p. A11).
11. The researchers used the Emotional Competence Inventory (ECI), a standard measure of emotional and social competence.
12. Hopkins and Bilmoria (2008).
13. Kerr, Garvin, and Heaton (2006). The EI test was the Mayer-Salovey-Caruso Emotional Intelligence Test (MSCEIT), one of the best-known and most respected measures of EI.
14. McClelland (1998).
15. Rosete (2007).
16. Bar-On, Handley, and Fund (2005).
17. Miao, Humphrey, and Qian (2016). The study was based on a meta-analysis, a statistical technique for pooling the results of numerous independent studies. The researchers found the correlation between a leader's EI and followers' job

satisfaction remained significant even when cognitive intelligence and personality were controlled for. It also was present no matter what measure or model of emotional intelligence was used.

18. Bhalerao and Kumar (2016).

19. Skakon, Nielsen, Borg, and Guzman (2010). See also Nielsen, Randall, Yarker, and Brenner (2008); Rasulzada, Dackert, and Johansson (2003).

20. Scott, Colquitt, Paddock, and Judge (2010).

21. Bryant (2011, July 7, p. 14).

22. Personal communication, November 28, 2017.

23. Many experts believe that influencing others is ultimately what leadership is all about. Two prominent leadership researchers put it succinctly when they defined leadership as "a process of *motivating* people to work together collaboratively to accomplish great things [emphasis added]" (Vroom & Jago, 2007, p. 218). See also Zaccaro (2002).

24. For more on this, see French and Raven's (1959) classic work on different bases of power and influence in groups.

25. As S. E. Murphy (2002) wrote, "Those people who feel that they are truly understood may be more likely to listen to the leader's ideas and implement his or her plans" (p. 175).

26. Bryant (2010, August 25).

27. Formal leaders are not the only ones in an organization who need to gain the trust of others in order to influence them. As one HR executive pointed out, "As organizations develop more distributed leadership models (where there are fewer formal leaders), individuals will increasingly need to be able to listen to and leverage the strengths and perspectives of many others who possess more domain specific expertise" (Engholm, personal communication, November 16, 2017).

28. Pescosolido (2002, p. 593)

29. Pescosolido (2002, p. 595).

30. S. E. Murphy (2002, p. 174). Like charisma, transformational leadership often involves the use of emotional appeals to help followers reach new levels of achievement (Burns, 1978). Transformational leaders develop clear and compelling visions, and they inspire their followers to work toward those visions through their use of language, storytelling, and other communication devices (Bass, 2002). Transformational leaders also are sensitive to their followers' needs. They can identify those needs and act in ways that inspire dedication and enthusiasm for the task. Several studies have found a link between transformational leadership and emotional intelligence. For a comprehensive review, see the meta-analysis by Harms and Credé (2010).

31. Bryant (2011, March 13).

32. Sutton (2010).

33. This view of leadership as involving two distinct dimensions, one "hard" and the other "soft," has a long history in research and theory. See, for instance, the research on task-oriented versus person-oriented leaders (Bass, 1981).

34. For a thoughtful and systematic consideration of how stress and emotion influence decision-making, see Mann (1992). Thompson (2010) also provides a useful perspective on the topic.

35. A number of leadership theorists have suggested that leaders can be both strong and caring. Kaplan (1996) has presented a useful way of thinking about the issue in a book written for a general audience.

36. A large meta-analysis found that cognitive intelligence accounted for about 8% of the variability in leaders' performance (Judge, Colbert, & Ilies, 2004).

37. Several members at the meeting disagreed. They asserted that if a leader behaves in a selfish way that harms others or the leader's organization, then he must be deficient in some aspect of EI. As the discussion continued, it became clear that the two sides were basing their positions on different models of EI. Those who argued that leaders could use their EI in harmful ways were thinking of the four basic EI abilities that constitute the Mayer-Salovey-Caruso model (emotion perception, use, understanding, and management). Those who argued the other position were thinking of the models that included not only those basic abilities but also traits linked to positive values such as empathy and teamwork.

38. Our colleague Richard Boyatzis initially suggested this distinction to us.

39. Some of the leading emotions researchers have made a similar point. For example, Barrett and Salovey (2002) predicted that while the field will benefit from research on the assessment of individual differences in EI abilities, it is also valuable to acquire a "deeper understanding of the processes that subserve these different skills" (p. 7). Caruso and Salovey (2004) went on to show how managers can use the EI abilities as a tool for dealing with issues, rather than a set of static traits. George (2000) provided a good theoretical analysis of how emotional abilities can be valuable for a variety of leadership functions. More recently, Côté (2013) proposed that we should now study how people use emotional intelligence to achieve goals and make decisions: "What do people do on a day-to-day basis when they use their EI?" Researchers and theorists interested in leadership also have advocated for a "functional, process-oriented" approach rather than one focusing on traits or behaviors. A notable example is the work of Hackman and Wageman (2005, 2007).

Focus on Feeling

L ike many of the outstanding leaders we studied, Cynthia, the head of a large engineering firm, had to steer her company through the Great Recession of 2008. When we interviewed her, she noted that the senior leadership team had "some difficult conversations" during those years. The mood during their meetings was often somber. One day, Cynthia realized that the senior leaders were carrying that tone with them back to their work groups after the meetings. "I noticed that people were leaving the room with long faces," she said. Cynthia was concerned about the impact this would have on the morale and motivation of the employees. Understanding that people look to the leader to get their cue on how they are doing, she worried that these expressions would communicate a sense of doom about the company to the rest of the employees. So at the next meeting, she said to the team, "Look, guys, the next time we leave this room, smile like the sun is shining." Although some people might question whether smiling after a difficult meeting was the best way to handle the situation, Cynthia had accurately identified an emotional pattern that could have adverse consequences for the organization.

As we spent time talking with Cynthia about how she handled this incident and others, it became apparent that she was *continually monitoring the emotional climate of meetings and other interactions*; this strategy, along with others that made use of her emotional intelligence, helped her lead her company through difficult times. Many other leaders used this strategy as well.[1]

STRATEGY 1: MONITOR THE EMOTIONAL CLIMATE

Most of the outstanding leaders were not just aware of their emotions or skillful in identifying what emotions other people are experiencing. They actively looked for subtle signs of emotion in order to influence the course of events. It was an active, purposeful process, and when they detected a potential problem, such as discouragement among the top management team spilling over and infecting the rest of the employees, they took action.

BECOMING AWARE OF AN EMPLOYEE PROBLEM

As the leaders monitored the emotional climate of a group, they often became aware of how certain individuals within the group were adversely affecting that climate. For example, after the layoffs occurred in her company, Cynthia made a point of walking around the building to see how people were reacting. It was not long before she noticed that one person was particularly angry, and that anger was not abating. Cynthia said:

> She was generally a happy kind of person. But as I walked by her office, I noticed that her door was always half closed; and I thought, "That's unusual." And I could see the scowl on her face. I let it go a

day or so, and then I decided there was something wrong. So I went in to talk with her. And she said, "What do you want?" in an abrupt tone of voice. I said, "When are you going to stop being so angry with me?" And she said, "I'm not angry, I'm mad."

Cynthia then asked the employee if she wanted to talk about her feelings then or schedule another time. The employee answered, "I'm fine. I don't want to talk about it." Cynthia gently persisted, and eventually the employee opened up and talked about her concerns. Although their talk did not lead to any dramatic changes, it helped clear the air and improve their relationship. If Cynthia had not been monitoring the emotional climate closely, she might not have detected the change in this employee's feelings, which signaled that something was wrong.

Much of the information that we communicate to one another is done through our emotions. As little as 10% of interpersonal communication is conveyed through words alone.[2] The rest is conveyed nonverbally through gesture, tone of voice, and facial expression. And leaders ultimately succeed or fail based on how much good information they have. Monitoring the emotional climate thus is a savvy strategy for any leader.[3]

In monitoring the emotional climate of a group or an interpersonal interaction, the leaders needed to distinguish between *their* feelings and those of others. Many of us often assume that others will react to a situation the same way we do. If we act only based on how we are feeling, ignoring how others feel, we may make poor decisions that harm our relationships with others and dilute our ability to influence them. As Cynthia noted when discussing how she dealt with the layoffs in her company, "It's important to be aware of how you're going through it, but also to look at the faces of the people to see how they're going through the change." In her case, she was able to move quickly beyond her sadness about having to lay off valued employees and see a brighter future. However, as she continued to monitor the emotional climate, she realized that some of the remaining employees felt different. They found it more difficult to move forward and feel optimistic about the future. Cynthia used this insight to tone down her positive feelings and respond more empathically to the employees who still felt considerable anxiety and sadness about the layoffs.[4]

But Cynthia did not just monitor the emotional climate. Once she perceived that there was a potential problem, she acted on it. The same was true for the other leaders and the incidents they described. Monitoring the emotional climate on a continuous basis was just the beginning of an active process that involved decisive and effective action, usually sooner rather than later.

DETECTING A SIMMERING CONFLICT

Monitoring the climate can be especially helpful in detecting destructive conflicts within organizations. Michael, a division president in a large company that sells agricultural products, described how he was able to deal effectively with simmering conflicts over the company's new strategic direction by keeping his finger on the emotional pulse of his top management team. As the group discussed the proposed changes, Michael became aware that one person in particular did not agree with the new approach. While that person did not openly disagree during the meeting, Michael was able to detect the person's opposition because of subtle changes in his emotional demeanor (signs of such emotional changes might include shifting uneasily in his seat, becoming flushed, lack of eye contact, or a slight downturn of his mouth).

Once Michael detected signs suggesting that the person was not fully committed to the new strategic direction, he took the initiative by meeting one-on-one with the individual to discuss their differences. Michael began the meeting by sharing his observations of the other's behavior. He said, "Look, you're just sending all the signals that you're not with me on this, so let's talk about it. Tell me what you don't like about this, and tell me what you like about it. And then we will talk about where we're going and what we are going to do about that."

In this example, Michael identified underlying resistance by monitoring how members of his team were responding emotionally. When he identified an individual who seemed to have mixed feelings about the changes, he met with him and began the conversation by reflecting back what he had observed and what he thought it suggested about the individual's feelings. This approach opened up a constructive dialogue for addressing the conflict. Looking back at the incident, Michael said, "I think, from an 'emotional intelligence' aspect, being open with somebody so that they see you do recognize there is an issue, and that you are willing to work on that issue, to take it to the next level . . . I think that gains a huge amount of credibility."

Michael's example shows why, as a leader, one would want to monitor and then follow up on emotional cues with one's team. Doing so not only helps create alignment and improve work processes; it also helps leaders gain credibility with their employees by bringing to the forefront important but often hidden dynamics.

MONITORING THE EMOTIONAL CLIMATE OF A TEAM

In addition to boosting morale and managing strategic change, monitoring the emotional climate helped leaders to diagnose and deal with conflicts within teams. Julia, the senior vice president for human resources (HR) in a large, multinational pharmaceutical company, was the HR person supporting the top management team for sales earlier in her career. There were about 10 people on the team, all sales vice presidents, and they had worked together well in the past—in fact, they had been one of the top-performing teams in the company. But recently things had changed. In Julia's words, a new head of sales "was really stirring things up and calling into question what the sales team was doing. Also, the numbers were starting to not look so good and there was pressure to deliver the results." A few new members of the team also added to the strain.

As Julia continued to monitor the emotional climate of the group, she saw that the increased pressure was having negative effects. As she explained, "They were not supporting one another, not speaking well of each other outside the room. . . . But no one ever talked about their feelings." So Julia decided to act. She went to the team's leader and asked him for permission to meet with the team to help them deal more constructively with their problems. Because Julia had worked with the team leader and earned his trust, he agreed.

Julia met with the team and helped them to talk about the changes that had occurred in the group. As a result, the team developed new norms about how to support one another. According to Julia: "We spent almost two hours talking about this, and we ended up with some commitments about how we would behave in the room and outside the room, and how we would call people on it if we felt those commitments weren't being honored. And we agreed that once a month or so we would check in with each other and see how we are doing."

A lack of trust can be highly damaging for groups and organizations if it is not addressed. If Julia's team had not addressed their internal problems and become a more cohesive group, the consequences could have had a significant impact on the effectiveness of the whole organization. Fortunately, Julia was closely monitoring the emotional climate, and when she detected problems, she acted.

DETECTING THE ABSENCE OF POSITIVE EMOTION IN A TEAM

Monitoring the emotional climate often helps leaders detect negative emotions that could be warning signs of trouble, but detecting the absence of positive emotion also can be helpful, for it frequently points to untapped opportunities. In another incident involving the weekly meeting of Cynthia's leadership team, one of the members reported some good news, which was a significant change. This is how it happened, in Cynthia's words: "On Monday we track our weekly revenue, and recently we exceeded our target. Usually, we are just hitting it and barely scraping by, but we exceeded it." However, Cynthia noticed that there was not much reaction to the news. "I could see that for the group, it was like, 'Oh, all right, we exceeded it,' and they were going on to another topic." Cynthia recognized that the group was missing an opportunity to boost morale. So she stepped in and said, "You know, this is really good! Tell me how you did this." And as the team members began to talk about how they had accomplished the positive results, Cynthia could see them becoming "more animated" about their success.

Looking back on what happened, Cynthia said, "I had to draw them into feeling good . . . just saying it doesn't make it happen. You have to suck them into the energy as much as possible and recognize that you're doing it." Then she added, "Sometimes you have to raise the temperature a little bit even though it's not your style. . . . So I have to raise the temperature in how I'm communicating with them, raise the emotion level, and then bring it back down, in a controlled way."

Cynthia's story illustrates how the most effective leaders often do not just monitor the emotional climate in order to detect and fix problems, but also to take advantage of opportunities. Keeping a finger on a group's emotional pulse helps them to identify opportunities for positive change, as in the case of Cynthia's leadership team when they heard some rare good news.

HOW DO LEADERS MONITOR THE EMOTIONAL CLIMATE?

There were several ways in which the leaders used their emotional intelligence to monitor the emotional climate. In Cynthia's incident with the angry employee, she used physical clues such as the half-closed door that was usually opened. She also noticed nonverbal behavior such as a "scowl" on the person's face and an "abrupt" tone of voice. Michael looked at nonverbal behavior in order to monitor the emotional climate in his leadership team. "I'm a very visual person," he said. "I watch body language a lot, and you can tell when somebody's engaged or when they're passive-resistant. I can see it." When we asked other leaders how they monitored the emotional climate, they mentioned doing things such as "listening well," being conscious of "the length of time someone spoke about something," and noting "where someone was displaying energy and what he seemed curious about." One leader also mentioned "diagnosing how the conversation is going" and "paying attention to my own gut." The leaders thus looked for a variety of signs to help them monitor the emotional climate.

These stories also show that when the leaders detected signs of problems or possibilities, they did not just sit back and hope for the best. They acted. For instance, when Cynthia noticed that an employee's door was half closed, she could have walked past without doing anything. However, she took action by knocking on the door and beginning a difficult conversation. She did not let it go and hope that things would improve on their own. Cynthia also demonstrated persistence and perseverance during the meeting with the employee. She did not back off when the employee initially tried to avoid a discussion of the problem.

Julia also demonstrated initiative when she went beyond her prescribed responsibilities to help her team deal with conflict and morale. She was not in a formal leadership position; as the team's generalist HR representative, she could have sat back and just observed the team members struggle to deal with their issues. Instead, she asked the team leader's permission to take charge of a meeting in order to have the team members engage in an unusual activity. Many of the other outstanding leaders we interviewed also demonstrated this kind of initiative. They did not simply observe the emotional climate; they actively looked for subtle signs of emotion in order to influence the course of events. And when they saw an opportunity or need, they acted.[5]

CONCLUSION

Monitoring the emotional climate seemed to be a useful strategy for many of the leaders we studied. However, some writers have suggested that emotional sensitivity can get in the way of effective leadership.[6] Leadership, they argue, requires decisive action, incisive analysis, and careful planning, and emotional sensitivity makes it more difficult for leaders to do these things effectively. What this view fails to consider, however, is that it is necessary for leaders to do both. In certain situations, it might be better for leaders to block out emotional awareness so they can concentrate on the task at hand. Examples might include officers leading soldiers in the midst of battle or surgeons directing their teams during a critical stage of an operation. On the other hand, there will be situations in which these same leaders need to monitor a group's emotional climate. Surgeons, for example, might miss some vital information, or have a real morale problem in their operating room team, if they do not monitor the team's emotional climate before and after the operation. Part of emotional intelligence is the ability to modulate emotional sensitivity depending on the situation.

There also will be times when leaders need to act decisively, plan calmly, *and* monitor the emotional pulse of a meeting or a relationship simultaneously. The outstanding leaders in our study had the facility to do so. In fact, what often made these leaders so effective was that their action and planning were *informed* by their continual monitoring of the emotional climate. It was thus one of their most useful strategies.

ACTIVITY 1.1: MONITORING THE EMOTIONAL CLIMATE
AT YOUR NEXT MEETING

The meeting room is one environment where leaders often find themselves spending countless hours analyzing, strategizing, and discussing important issues with others. Besides being a forum for discussing business matters, meetings can also provide leaders with valuable opportunities to hone their skills at monitoring the emotional environment within their organizations, as we learned from the cases presented in this chapter. It was during meetings that leaders like Cynthia, Julia, and Michael discovered important emotional clues that were linked to underlying issues within the organizations.

Your job as an emotionally intelligent leader is to take advantage of this opportunity. Make a point of observing an upcoming meeting. Block it off in your calendar as a meeting in which you will observe more and talk less. Jot down your observations soon after the meeting so you can recall what happened more easily when trying to make sense of the data. Here are a few prompts to get you started:

- What kind of nonverbal behavior do you notice?
- Do people seem distracted and uninterested? Positive and engaged?
- Is there anything that feels different to you than in previous meetings?
- Who is there and not there? Could it be that a person's absence might be related to how people are feeling in a group? Who arrives early and who arrives late? Where do people sit and with whom?
- What is being spoken about? What is *not* being spoken about?

Next, speak with a person who was at the meeting to test your observations. Ask open-ended questions so that you can capture a wide breadth of information. For example, you could simply ask, "What did you think of the meeting?" (*If you noticed a person who seemed particularly affected during the meeting, you may ask this question as a way to open a discussion about what you observed, but be careful that you are not communicating a sense of judgment or condemnation. As an emotional monitor, your task is to gather information about what may be affecting the emotional climate of the meeting.*) Let the person know that you appreciate his or her feedback, since it is valuable information that you might not otherwise have had.

Finally, after obtaining another perspective, reflect on your role and how it might be influencing what happened in the meeting. Generate some hunches as to what might be going on based on what you learned from both your observations and follow-up conversations, and use this information as the basis for positive change. For example, if you sensed a positive atmosphere in the meeting, how might you build on that? If, on the other hand, you detected something amiss on the part of an individual or the team, what steps could you take to begin dealing with the problem?

NOTES

1. Fifteen of the 25 leaders in the study used the strategy "Monitor the emotional climate" in at least one of the critical incidents they described. Of the 126 incidents described by the leaders during the interviews, 23 involved the use of this strategy.
2. Caruso and Salovey (2004).
3. Perkins (2000), in his fascinating study of the leadership skill displayed by the explorer Ernest Shackleton during his epic expedition in the Antarctic, highlighted how he continually monitored the emotional state of every team member to detect signs of anxiety or other potentially destructive emotional states.
4. Ury (1991), in writing about the role of emotion in negotiation and conflict management, suggests that we need to recognize not only what our opponents are doing but also what they are feeling.
5. Initiative is one of those emotional and social competencies linked to effective leadership. Dozens of competency studies have shown that initiative is often one of the competencies that most strongly differentiate between outstanding and average leaders (Boyatzis, 1982; Goleman, 1998; Spencer & Spencer, 1993).
6. Antonakis, Ashkanasy, and Dasborough (2009).

2

Let People Know How You Feel

A aron was the CEO of a large construction firm. He was a burly man who had risen to the top in an industry not known for "soft skills." So we were surprised when the first incident he described in our interview, the sudden collapse and death of his board chairman, was one in which Aaron's direct expression of his own sadness and grief in front of his employees played a prominent and positive role. Here is how he began his story: "The chairman of our company had started his presentation at a company meeting last December. After speaking for a few minutes, he had a heart attack and died. . . . It was quite an emotional experience. There were 96 people in the room when it happened, and the news quickly spread through the whole company."

The loss was especially hard for Aaron. He had been close to the chairman for many years; the chairman was Aaron's mentor and guide. "For me, it was the loss of a confidant. I could go into his office and complain, and he'd say, 'Yes, you're right.'" We asked Aaron how he handled the situation, and he replied:

I went to the hotel that night and talked with people. Then I addressed the whole company the next morning. And my message was, "Forget about work today. This was our family who we lost, our friend . . ." Then I said, "If you truly love anyone in your family, I suggest you tell them today because none of us knows when our time will come. . . . You might not be here tomorrow, or they may not be here. None of us have any control over that." So I addressed the people, we managed, we kept going, and the company didn't fall apart. We're as successful today as we were then . . . although I'm not sure I'm the same today.

One can imagine other ways in which the leader in this situation might respond. For example, he or she might minimize the expression of any emotion, briefly noting the loss and then encouraging people to get past it as quickly as possible. Aaron's approach, however, involved an open acknowledgment of the emotional impact the situation was having on everyone, including himself. In his remarks to the employees, he used the first-person plural: "This was *our* family who *we* lost, *our* friend," and "None of *us* knows when *our* time will come." Aaron's grief was palpable. He did not try to minimize it or hide it from his employees. Expressing those feelings revealed Aaron's own sense of vulnerability, which could have made the employees more anxious, but it also revealed his humanity. It reduced the distance between him and the rest of the employees, which ultimately strengthened their trust in him. The way in which Aaron handled the death of his company's chairman illustrated the second emotional intelligence strategy that many of our leaders used.

STRATEGY 2: EXPRESS YOUR FEELINGS TO MOTIVATE OTHERS

Evolutionary theorists believe that the expression of emotion serves an important adaptive function for many species, including our own. It motivates us and others to act in response to challenges or opportunities. It also serves as an important signaling system;[1] knowing how the boss feels when he or she comes in at the beginning of the day can be valuable information for everyone in the group!

Suppressing our emotions can be costly in a number of ways. Perhaps most important, it can impede the development of positive relationships with others. As James Gross of Stanford University noted, "One reason we're so attuned to others' emotions is that when it's a real emotion, it tells us something important about what matters to that person. When it's suppressed or toned down, people think, 'Damn it, you're not like us, you don't care about the same things we do.'"[2] Indeed, in one study, college students who scored high on a measure of emotion suppression found it harder to make friends.[3]

A leader's emotional expression also sets the tone for a group and can influence the group's effectiveness. For instance, imagine that you are in a group that has been asked to come up with a good plan for distributing bonuses to employees in a fictitious organization. The leader of your group is positive and upbeat. Your friend is in another group with the same task, but the leader in her group is dour and glum. Which of you do you think will have a more positive experience? Also, which group will work better together as a group? And which group will come up with a better plan?

Organizational researcher Sigal Barsade conducted a classic study that closely resembled this imaginary scenario.[4] She randomly assigned participants to four types of groups. In each group there was the same trained confederate (a professional actor). The confederate in the first type of group was cheerful and enthusiastic. In the second condition he was warm and serene. In the third, the confederate was hostile and irritable. And in the fourth he was depressed and sluggish. In all the groups, the confederate emerged early on as the informal leader, as he had been instructed to do.

Barsade found that there was a strong "emotional contagion" effect, with group members "catching" the informal leader's mood (though the effect was weaker when the leader was depressed). Also, there was more cooperation and less conflict in the groups that had a positive leader. The most intriguing finding, however, was that the groups with an emotionally upbeat leader performed better on the assigned task. In sum, the mood of a group made a difference in its effectiveness, and the group leader's expression of emotion could determine the group's mood.

Emotion expression is what sets charismatic leaders apart from others,[5] and it plays an important role in group development, persuasion, and psychological safety.[6] Expressing emotions even can help leaders remember important details. In one study, people were shown an upsetting movie. Some of the people were asked to suppress their emotions. Afterward the viewers were given a test on what they saw. Those who tried to suppress their emotions remembered fewer details.[7] Suppressing emotion also uses energy, and this energy gets siphoned away from problem-solving.[8]

STRENGTHENING POSITIVE RELATIONS
BY EXPRESSING SORROW

The leaders in our study often seemed to express sorrow or sadness as a strategy to motivate others and develop positive relationships.[9] Like Aaron, they often did so when helping their employees deal with a tragic, personal loss. Yolanda, the director of training and development for a large clothing manufacturer, described an incident in which a member of her team had a son who was killed in an automobile accident. The team was close-knit, so the news was upsetting for everyone. It was many weeks before the team member finally returned to work, but while she was away Yolanda reached out to her, calling and visiting often. Yolanda admitted that she had been nervous because she did not know exactly how to handle the situation. However, she did not withdraw. In her role as leader and mentor, Yolanda often checked in to see how her teammate was doing. Those visits could be emotional: "It's really hard for her, and I feel it," said Yolanda. "So sometimes we cry."

There are no clear rules for how a leader should deal with a situation like this. Some leaders seem to believe that one should maintain a businesslike demeanor to avoid undermining one's authority or making a bad situation worse. They might even believe that such a distanced approach will help the grieving employee to "get over it" more quickly. It is true that organizational leaders should not act like personal friends, psychotherapists, or members of the clergy. But Yolanda believed that, as leader of the group, part of her responsibility is to help her people function at an optimal level because helping one person to function helps everyone to function.

However, the most helpful way for the leader to express emotion varies with the situation and cultural context. In this particular situation, it appeared to be appropriate for Yolanda to cry with her bereaved team member when they were alone together away from the office. However, crying would probably not be very helpful during a meeting back at work to discuss the new strategic plan for the company, even if all the team members were upset about the changes. Expressing those feelings in other ways, however, might help the group to move on and deal with the situation most effectively.

Yolanda's approach seemed to receive vindication when, after some time had passed, the teammate told her what her support had meant to her. She said, "You have been perfect. . . . You kept the connection, and I know you're there."

Like many of the other leaders we studied, Yolanda did not try to minimize the emotions stirred up by this situation. She actively engaged with those emotions and with those who were feeling them. She allowed herself to feel the emotions and then used the emotions to guide her own actions. At the same time, she needed to manage those emotions so that she was not overwhelmed by them. Also, she needed to be aware at some level of the norms for expressing emotion in her organization. If her emotionality was excessive by those standards, the result could have been less positive.[10] Emotional intelligence ultimately involves the skillful combination of all the core abilities (emotion awareness, expression, understanding, and management).

EXPRESSING ONE'S FEELINGS TO HELP EMPLOYEES COPE WITH LAYOFFS

Layoffs represent a different kind of loss, and some of the leaders found that openly expressing their own feelings seemed to help the remaining employees to cope. Cynthia, the head of a large engineering firm, was one of those leaders. After the firm laid off about 10% of its employees, she met with the remaining ones in an all-company meeting. Rather than hold back her feelings, she expressed them:

> During the meeting, the message was, "Here's what we did. It sucked. It wasn't fun. We didn't do it because these were bad people. We did it to align the work and the workforce. Here's where we would have been if we had not done it, and here's where we are going to be instead." So it was kind of trying to spend some time feeling emotion about what the events were, but then helping them understand and taking them to the same place emotionally by giving them a compelling story. . . . *It involved helping people manage their emotions by doing the same with them.*

As Cynthia noted, sharing with her employees how she felt about the layoffs was an important part of the healing process. She helped her employees manage their emotions by sharing her own in a direct but modulated way. However, Cynthia emphasized that it was equally important to help everyone move on by expressing a more hopeful perspective on the situation. So, after spending some time talking about her own feelings and allowing others to talk about theirs, Cynthia spoke more optimistically about the future. There was a balance between expressing negative emotion (sadness, sorrow, loss) with more positive emotion (hope, optimism), and striking this balance made the expression of emotion especially helpful in this situation.

In addition to the balance in emotional tone, there also was a balance between thinking and feeling. After Cynthia shared her feelings with the group, she shifted to a more analytical mode. She presented charts and numbers showing where the company would have been financially if it had not implemented the layoffs and where it would be because of the layoffs. Carefully balancing feeling with thinking in this way was an example of expressing emotion in an emotionally intelligent way.

The process Cynthia went through in announcing the layoffs was even more emotionally intelligent because as the changes occurred she continually monitored the emotional climate to ensure that her presentation of the situation was having the desired effect on her employees. After describing how she handled the meeting, she said, "And it's important to be aware of how you're going through it, but also to look at the faces of the people to see how they're going through the change."

Analyzing what Cynthia did at the meeting in this way is somewhat misleading because it makes it seem as though it was a calculated, mechanical performance. However, if it had been, it probably would not have been effective. In fact, it might have made matters worse. Although there was some calculation, in that Cynthia planned to start her presentation by discussing her own negative feelings and then move on to a more positive view based on rational analysis, once the presentation began she allowed herself to "talk from the heart." The feelings she expressed were real feelings, and she expressed them authentically.

Cynthia continued to express her own feelings about the layoffs during the next few weeks in one-on-one discussions with employees. For instance, when she met with an employee who was upset about how the layoffs were handled, Cynthia allowed the employee to "ventilate" and then told the employee what her own feelings were about what happened. Cynthia's expression of her own emotions helped the employee express her feelings more openly and directly, which helped the employee better manage her emotions. Also, because Cynthia's feelings were similar to the employee's, expressing those feelings helped break down the barriers that had developed between Cynthia and the employee.

EXPRESSING FEELINGS TO INSPIRE OTHERS AT A TOWN HALL MEETING

Layoffs can be harmful for morale in any organization, but the leaders we studied often tried to boost morale even when there was not a specific event. And openly expressing their own emotions played a significant role. For example, Aaron, who held several town hall meetings each year, described one in which he sought to inspire his employees by beginning with a story about the enthusiasm and dedication displayed by one of their work crews:

> The week before, I had gone to two job-site meetings at 6:00 a.m. in New York City, and I opened up my presentation [at the town hall] by referring to these meetings. I said, "These people are out there at a planning meeting at 6:00 in the morning every day! They do this *every* day! And they don't live in New York. And they don't leave at 3:30 in the afternoon either. And what really impressed me was that there was a lot of enthusiasm." I opened up my presentation with this, and I got tremendous feedback.

Like Cynthia, Aaron was telling a "compelling story" in order to fire up his employees. In this case, it was based on an actual event that had occurred in the recent past rather than a vision of the future. And in both cases, it was not just a picture or story that motivated others, but also the leader's own feelings and the moving way in which he or she expressed them during the telling of the story. If Aaron had not been "really impressed" by what he saw at those 6:00 a.m. planning meetings, and if he had not been able to express his feelings openly as he told his staff about what he had seen, it would not have had much impact on the enthusiasm and commitment of his listeners.[11]

Expressing emotion was especially important when leaders apologized for mistakes they had made. Many political and business leaders seem to have learned from their coaches that when they make a mistake, the best thing to do is apologize. However, too often those apologies seem hollow. The leaders show little emotion, and they use statements such as "Mistakes were made," which suggest little remorse or sense of personal responsibility on the leader's part. An effective apology is deeply personal and not just a prescribed attempt to defuse a difficult situation or gain acceptance. Outstanding leaders do not spend lots of time apologizing; but when they do apologize, it is effective because it comes from the heart.

BUT WHAT ABOUT ANGER? HOW ONE LEADER
USED IT EFFECTIVELY

We have seen that the leaders achieved important outcomes by expressing negative emotions such as sorrow and regret, as well as positive ones such as admiration and enthusiasm. But what about anger? Expressing anger seems to be more complicated. Becoming angry and showing it can often get leaders in trouble. However, a few of the incidents suggested that expressing anger can sometimes be adaptive if leaders do it in an emotionally intelligent way. Julia, the senior vice president of HR for a large pharmaceutical company, described one such incident. A manager in her company was planning to eliminate the job of someone who Julia thought was a good contributor and a talented person. Therefore, she asked two of her HR staff to talk with the employee and encourage him to take a job in another part of the company. "So I asked my HR people about doing this at least three times, and finally about a week later I asked again, 'So whatever happened to Alan?' They said, 'Well, we're waiting to write the job description, and . . .' It was like all this bureaucratic stuff! So I said, 'Stop! This is our employee, and I don't know why you're dragging it out!' And after that it got done in a day. It was a very frustrating thing for me."

This leader communicated her exasperation in a clear, direct way; as a result, the bureaucratic logjam was broken. Her brief, focused expression of anger also communicated the importance of caring and compassion when dealing with employees more generally. The underlying message was that bureaucratic procedure should not be allowed to get in the way of treating employees humanely. This example suggests that the expression of anger can help leaders to influence others and achieve their goals; however, it also points to some of the factors that determine whether the expression of anger will be effective or counterproductive. Julia's positive relationship with her staff, and their long history of working together, made Julia's outburst particularly effective and minimized negative consequences. The same outburst from a leader who was perceived in a less positive way might not have worked as well.[12]

TIPS FOR EXPRESSING EMOTIONS EFFECTIVELY

Even with positive emotions, the way in which a leader expresses them can make a big difference in how effective they are. Unfortunately, describing how the leaders expressed emotion effectively in a situation can be difficult. It is like trying to describe in words how a world-class golfer swings her club or how a violin virtuoso moves his bow across the strings. Nevertheless, some of the leaders we interviewed suggested a few of the elements that helped them.

Bruce, the superintendent of a suburban school district, described how he set the tone during his meeting with the teachers at the beginning of the year. "I don't script anything. . . . As I'm talking, I can usually come up with the right words to bring everyone together. I don't write them down. That doesn't work for me. I have to speak from the heart."

However, Bruce did suggest that a certain amount of thought and planning helped. He said, "I'm always conscious of the feeling tone any time I give a talk or in anything I write. I'll even ask a couple of people to check it for feeling tone." It is not as though Bruce can turn his feelings on or off, but he can think ahead about the "right tone to set" in a forthcoming situation and how strongly he wants to express his feelings as opposed to modulate them. Then, when the time is right, he can call on the right feelings and express them in a way that moves others.[13] Thus, while the feelings Bruce expresses during those important speeches are genuine, mental preparation plays a role. Like all emotionally intelligent action, it involves both the thinking parts of the brain and the feeling parts.[14]

Bruce's comments also suggest that to express emotion effectively, we need to be comfortable with the idea of doing so. We have to believe that expressing emotion is "OK" rather than something to avoid. Attitude is as important as technique. Bruce was able to inspire people by expressing his feelings because he believed it was OK to do so. In fact, he saw "setting the right feeling tone" as an important part of his job. Leaders who believe it is better for one in their position to avoid emotional displays, or who are unsure about it, will probably not be able to express emotion effectively.

Aaron's story about his visit to a work crew at 6 a.m. illustrates how sharing a compelling story can help leaders to express emotions effectively. Dorothy, the head of a small, nonprofit social services agency, also used stories to help her express emotions in ways that inspired others. She said, "It's really important to share the enthusiasm, excitement, and sense of urgency." She then described a presentation she made recently to a potential funder. Initially, she was not feeling very enthusiastic because she was having surgery the next day. She explained, "It was the last thing I wanted to do. Yet, as I spoke with them and began to talk about the families we serve and the needs of the clients we have, I could just see them nodding and saying things under their breath like, 'That's what it's all about' or 'That sounds great.' The same thing happens when I talk to the board."

When Dorothy told her stories about clients they had helped, and she saw how people in the audience were moved by those stories, she became even more moved herself. It was not just the stories that increased her enthusiasm and passion. Seeing the expression of positive emotion in her listeners as they responded to these stories helped increase Dorothy's enthusiasm. It was a dynamic and reciprocal process, a "virtuous cycle" in which the leader's emotions spread to others and then the others' emotions reinforced the leader.[15]

Of all the emotions leaders can express, enthusiasm is often the most powerful and effective. Amy Gutmann, the president of the University of Pennsylvania, said that she learned this from "every excellent teacher" she has ever had. She quoted Emerson, who wrote, "Nothing great was ever achieved without enthusiasm."[16] Leaders who understand this and are able to generate and maintain enthusiasm in themselves are at an advantage.

Dorothy emphasized that her enthusiasm was not something that she planned or manufactured in a calculated way. "I don't think of my passion as 'managing emotion.' It just comes out." However, what was calculated was using stories to help increase her enthusiasm and make it infectious. She understood that those stories, when told the right way, would have that effect. But once she began to tell the stories, she could just let the emotional part of her brain do the rest.

Although it is especially effective to use one's own experiences, leaders often must go out and look for the stories. When Aaron went to observe the meeting at a work site early in the morning, he placed himself in a situation that provided a powerful story, which he later shared with the rest of his company. Although he might have referred to the meeting in his speech without actually going there and participating in it, he probably would not have been as inspired and thus would not have had as much feeling when he told the story at the town hall meeting. The lesson for leaders who wish to express emotion in order to motivate others is to create or look for an effective stimulus, such as a personal or work-related story, and then allow the emotion it stimulates to come out in one's words and actions.[17]

CONCLUSION: SHOULD LEADERS ALWAYS SHOW HOW THEY ARE FEELING?

Many organizational leaders are hesitant to express how they feel, especially when those feelings are negative. They believe that it might undermine rational, objective action and threaten the order and predictability that are essential for the smooth functioning of groups and organizations. Some leaders also might worry that expressing their feelings could undermine their authority. Even some of the leaders in our study suggested that in crisis situations it is important for them to appear calm and not let others think that they are upset. So what should a leader do in such situations?

Trying to appear calm by denying or minimizing the challenges that the leader and his or her group faces probably will not work. A better approach is for leaders to acknowledge those challenges and to empathize with how others may be feeling about them while maintaining a calm composure, as Cynthia tried to do in discussing the layoffs with her employees. Leaders ideally should maintain an even keel in order to help others manage their own emotions. In short, it is usually better for leaders to express emotion but maintain control.

Sometimes, however, even losing control emotionally in the presence of others can be innocuous and may even have a positive impact. For example, we once saw a leader lose his customary composure and begin to weep when he announced the death of a close friend and colleague. That action did not in any way undermine his authority or affect others in a negative way. If anything, it made him seem more human, which increased the respect and loyalty that others felt toward him. So what set this situation apart? When is it OK for leaders to become momentarily overwhelmed by their emotions when they express them?

In this situation, and others we can think of, the type of emotion may be an important factor. Becoming overcome by the emotion when expressing sadness may ultimately have a positive effect, but becoming overcome by anger or fear may be deleterious. The strength and duration of the emotion and its expression also seem to be important. In our example, the leader briefly paused as a few tears rolled down his face. He clearly was upset. He clearly was crying. But it was a gentle weeping, not an earth-shaking sob. For a moment, he could not continue. But then he regained control, and within a few minutes he was back to his normal self. One final factor is how the leader is viewed by the group. In this case, the group members had known the leader for a long time. They knew him well and respected him. And they had seen him deal effectively with highly stressful situations in the past. As a result, his momentary loss of control as he expressed his emotions did not have a negative impact; if anything, it made his group feel even more loyal and committed.[18]

ACTIVITY 2.1: EXPRESSING EMOTIONS AND INFLUENCING OTHERS THROUGH STORYTELLING

There is tremendous power in a story. Leaders like Aaron and Dorothy found that storytelling can be a compelling way to convey emotion on many levels. It allows another person insight into our inner emotional life and what makes life meaningful, thus creating opportunities for connection. Storytelling can also be a persuasive tool to inspire others to action. The following exercise is meant to help you think about how to use your emotional experiences in the form of a story as a way to connect with and move others.

Instructions

1. Identify a person or a group of people whom you would like to inspire or help move in a particular direction.
2. Think about an experience that has had a strong emotional impact on you (either because it happened to you or you observed it) and that reflects the passion for an issue or event that you are trying to get others to share.
3. Write down how you might use that experience to formulate a story that will inspire others in their thinking or actions
4. To get you started thinking from a storytelling perspective, you might begin thinking about the experience in story form: How did it start? Who were the main characters? What happened? What problems or barriers were overcome? How did it end? What was the moral of the story—what did this experience show or teach you?

Remember that a story is something that captures people's imagination and attention, so it shouldn't be longwinded or preachy. It doesn't even have to be about dramatic events. For example, Aaron told a story based on an everyday experience on the job site. Taking your audience on a journey that has meaning for you, particularly as it relates to overcoming barriers or difficulties, is what invests them in your story. So give it a try—you can always give it a test run with someone you trust and see what kind of reaction you inspire!

ACTIVITY 2.2: WRITING TO EXPRESS YOUR EMOTIONS

Expressive writing is a private kind of writing that forces us to ask ourselves why and how we feel the way we do without input or judgment from others.[19] Marian, a VP of a large international chemical company, was one of the participants in this research who used writing to "say boldly what is happening" in herself and to move her thinking in a more linear direction. Extensive research on expressive writing has shown it to be a powerful tool in improving mental and physical health, such as immune response, inflammation, anxiety, and chronic pain. It has also been shown to benefit learning and job functioning.

The goal of this activity is to help you become more comfortable identifying and expressing the emotions you are experiencing. Here are some things to remember about expressive writing:

- There are no rules.
- Don't worry about grammar or spelling.
- You write only for yourself.
- Silence the inner critic and let go.

Instructions

Make a promise to yourself that you will write for 15 minutes a day at least four times a week. Write continuously for those 15 minutes about your deepest emotions and thoughts from recent past events, positive or negative, regardless of where you experienced them (i.e., home, work, etc.). The important goal is to focus on what your feelings are and why you feel that way in an honest and uncensored way. You also might write about how these emotions influence your relationships, your goals, and your dreams.

Just a Little Side Note: Writing this way may be a new experience and a bit uncomfortable at first. You may even feel a little sad after writing about a troubling experience. This is normal, and those feelings usually disappear within a few hours. Feel free to switch topics or stop writing for a while. Over time, though, you should begin to notice certain themes or patterns that may give you a new perspective on situations, feelings, and relationships.

ACTIVITY 2.3: GETTING TO KNOW YOUR
EMOTIONAL FINGERPRINT

How you express emotions is as unique as your fingerprint. We all have different abilities and comfort levels when it comes to letting others know how we feel. While some of us might shy away from expressing emotions, others might feel so comfortable that they express perhaps too much. The same might hold true when it comes to certain kinds of emotion. For example, expressing negative emotions may be easier for some people than expressing positive ones, and vice versa.

The following exercise is meant to help you "think" about the various factors that influence how you go about expressing your emotions. Feel free to write down your answers and discuss with a trusted friend.

- What is your attitude toward emotion?
- Which feelings are you comfortable expressing at work?
  At home?
- Which feelings are you not comfortable expressing at work?
  At home?
- When you do express your emotions, how have others reacted?
  Why do you think they reacted that way?
- If there was one emotion you wish you could better express, what would it be?

If there was an emotion that you wish you were better at expressing, look for role models around you who express that emotion well. (You may even look for actors and actresses on television or on film who portray the emotion particularly well.) What do they do that makes them effective at expressing that emotion? Take note of your observations and see if there is something in the way they express an emotion that you might be willing to try. You may just discover something new about yourself!

NOTES

1. Caruso and Salovey (2004); Darwin (1872).
2. Quoted in Carey (2010, p. 1).
3. Cited in Carey (2010).
4. Barsade (2002).
5. Sy, Horton, and Riggio (2018) recently proposed a model of charisma that "situates emotion as the primary variable in the charismatic process" (from the abstract). See also Bono and Ilies (2006); Gooty, Connelly, Griffith, and Gupta (2010).
6. For the link between group development and emotion expression, see Bennis and Shepard (1956). Mackie, Asuncion, and Rosselli (1992) discussed the impact of emotion expression on persuasion within a group, and Edmondson (1999) has discussed the role of emotion expression in creating a sense of psychological safety within a group. Smollan and Parry (2011) propose that "to engage followers in change" leaders "should inject emotion into their communications" (p. 441).
7. Richards and Gross (2000).
8. Caruso and Salovey (2004).
9. Altogether, 10 of the leaders described 17 incidents in which they used expressing emotion as a strategy.
10. Lindebaum and Cassell (2012) have pointed out that expressing feelings, especially certain kinds of feelings in certain contexts, may undermine a leader's credibility. They suggest that to be effective, leaders need to be aware of cultural norms concerning the expression of emotion and then shape their own behavior accordingly.
11. S. E. Murphy (2002) has noted that effective leaders influence others through the "creative use of words that paint a compelling vision of the future for the organization or work group" (p. 174).
12. Several recent studies have helped identify the conditions in which the expression of anger by a leader is likely to have positive consequences (Geddes & Callister, 2007; Hess, 2014; Lindebaum, Jordan, & Morris, 2015; Van Kleef, 2014). Parrott (2002) suggested that to be useful, negative emotions need to "appear under the right circumstances, be expressed in ways that are productive in the current situation, be regulated so that their intensity and manifestations are appropriate, and be restrained" (pp. 341–342) when they are not helpful.
13. Sarason (1999) has proposed that teaching is, among other things, a "performing art." The same could be said of leading others.
14. Hochschild (1983) has used the term *emotional labor* to describe situations in which a worker's job requires him or her to feel and express certain emotions in certain situations. Her work, and that of others, has usually suggested that emotional labor is stressful for the worker as well as duplicitous. However, Hochschild distinguished between "surface acting," in which workers change their outward display of emotion without changing their inner feelings, and "deep acting," which involves changing the way one actually feels and then expressing those feelings spontaneously. Ashforth and Humphrey (1993) suggested a third way in which workers can perform emotional labor, which they called "genuine emotional labor."

In this third condition, a worker's genuine, spontaneous feelings are aligned with the requirements of the job. The leaders in our study seemed to use either deep acting or genuine emotional labor.

15. A cycle is "virtuous" if the mutually reinforcing outcomes are positive; it is "vicious" when the results are negative.

16. Bryant (2011, June 19).

17. Many successful political leaders have been particularly adept at expressing emotions effectively. Theodore Roosevelt is a good example of one who used this ability to change opinions and inspire others to do more than they would otherwise. See Goodwin (2013).

18. Too much emotional expression can become a problem. Although many people believe that venting their emotion helps them feel better and gain control, the research suggests the opposite. Catharsis usually does not help: The more one vents, the worse one feels. See Bushman (2002).

19. This activity is based on Pennebaker and Smith's (2016) research and work, as described in their book.

3

What Is Your Impact on Others?

James was a senior vice president in a large consulting practice where one of the most important divisions was undergoing some intense regulatory scrutiny. Just as it was about to enter a particularly critical stage, the division head became ill. As James monitored the emotional climate of the leadership group (*Strategy 1*), he noted that there was "a lot of angst and unease because there was uncertainty around how long the person would be out. Would it be a couple of days? A couple of weeks? People were pretty well panicked because we were right in the throes of this regulatory challenge."

As he considered how his actions might help the staff deal with these feelings, James realized that making himself physically present to run the division temporarily would help reduce the uncertainty and stress. He explained:

> I felt I needed to interject myself to help them get through it, even if I didn't know the subject matter. I needed to give them

advice and counsel and inspiration. So I set myself up in one of the conference rooms, and we just worked on everything together. I said, "Whatever needs to be done, whatever we have to do, we're going to do it together. None of it is beneath us." My intent was to really assure them that we're going to be able to get through this.

James also recognized that it was crucial for him to keep his emotions in check and not let others see his own anxiety about the situation:

You can't let the people see you sweat. . . . If they see me feeling panicked or stressed or frenzied, they're never going to be able to feel like they can get it done. If I went in there panicked and overwhelmed, the others would have become more panicked. They would have felt like, "Oh my god, this guy's the boss's boss; and he comes in and can't help us. We're in a lot of trouble!" So I felt I had to demonstrate to them that, while it's not an ideal situation, I think we're up to it.

Because he understood how his own behavior would influence others, James was able to guide the team successfully through the completion of the project.[1]

STRATEGY 3: CONSIDER HOW YOUR OWN BEHAVIOR
INFLUENCES OTHERS' EMOTIONS

A leader's emotions and actions influence others constantly and in numerous ways. For instance, imagine a manager who presents a plan to her subordinates at a meeting. She wants their honest feedback and says so. However, if she is anxious about receiving negative feedback, it is likely that her subordinates will pick up on that feeling, and they will withhold or censor their feedback for both her sake and their own.

Anger in a leader can inhibit communication even more than anxiety. Cynthia, the CEO of a large engineering firm, described what happened when their former CEO was in a bad mood:

> When he had a bad day, you definitely knew it; and it affected everybody. If he didn't like something you said, he would rip into you. And while he was fine about that and could move on after five minutes, the other people in the group couldn't. So we found ourselves trying to gauge where he was emotionally before sharing information with him, and that wasn't a good thing. If there is an issue an employee has and they need your help, but they can't approach you right away, the problem just multiplies by the time it gets to you.

Cynthia then went on to describe how the CEO would react when something went wrong:

> If something went wrong, he would go from whatever mood he was in to "What did you do wrong!?" You know, like a client calls with a problem, and in the CEO's mind, automatically the employee was wrong. . . . As a leader you need to be more sensitive in the way you address the problem with the employee. Even when the employee has done something wrong, do you want him to stay down or do you want him to learn from the experience and move on?

When leaders become angry, they tend to discourage their subordinates from sharing valuable information with them. And when leaders have incomplete or distorted communication, they might risk making poor decisions. The result? Small problems become big ones.

Many leaders do recognize the importance of open channels of communication, and they want their employees to feel free to share ideas with them. As Robin Domeniconi, senior vice president and chief brand officer for the Elle Group, told a reporter, "I want to be challenged. I want to encourage debate so we can arrive at the right decision."[2] And Amy Gutmann, the president of the University of Pennsylvania, told the same reporter, "It's important to get feedback and to be open to the wild and crazy ideas, even if you're not going to pursue but a fraction of them."[3]

For many decades, the conventional wisdom was that emotion has no place in the work world, and the ideal leader is one who is rational and unemotional.[4] However, the reality is that emotion is inevitable when a group of people come together for an extended period to work on challenging tasks; if used effectively, a leader's moods and emotions can be a plus rather than a minus.

USING EMOTIONAL CONTAGION TO INFLUENCE OTHERS

Outstanding leaders intuitively understand the research on *emotional contagion* and how a leader can use it to influence the mood and performance of a group.[5] Several years ago, one of us interviewed an unusually effective public school principal as part of a study on school change.[6] Her school was located in a poor neighborhood made up almost completely of families from disadvantaged minority groups. Nevertheless, her students excelled, and she had won several awards for her accomplishments as an educational leader and reformer. At one point in the interview, as she was trying to describe why she had been so successful, she said that she had learned over the years that the teachers and staff can sense how she is feeling as soon as she walks into the building in the morning, and those feelings spread through the school like wildfire. Therefore, every morning when she arrives at school, she pauses after she parks her car to check on her feelings before entering the building. If she senses that she is feeling down, she focuses on changing her mood and does not go into the building until she feels cheerful and enthusiastic about starting the day.

Many of the leaders in our study also understood that their emotions could affect groups in beneficial ways, and they used this insight to engage and motivate the members of their teams. As a district manager for the state's child protective services agency, Clarence was particularly aware of how his feelings and actions affected his staff. One morning he woke up and, as was his custom, turned on the morning news while he got ready to go to work. What he saw sent a chill up his spine. The screen was filled with gruesome words and images about a mother who, a few hours earlier, had murdered her 2-year-old daughter and then killed herself, leaving behind several other children. What made the news even more disturbing for Clarence was that workers from his office had been working with the mother and thought she had been improving.

Clarence immediately realized the enormity of the emotional challenge that his workers now faced. As he put it, "For many people at the agency, this case was something that really hit close to home because it was not only one of the more horrific incidents of child abuse that the agency had ever witnessed, but also a complete shock since the mother and child had been making steady progress." Clarence went on to talk about the responsibility he felt for his staff. Based on his understanding of how his own feelings and actions would affect them, he believed that it was important for him to "check his own emotions at the door." In his words, "I went into manager mode. My own emotions? I had to deal with them after hours. When I was here, I had to assure my staff that we're going to get through this." Clarence finished dressing and got to the office as soon as he could. By the time he walked in, he had a detailed plan of action, and most of it focused on helping the staff deal with their feelings during the coming weeks. Clarence was an outstanding leader in part because he understood how his own feelings and actions would affect those with whom he worked, and he used this understanding to guide his actions as a leader.

Several other leaders talked about how important it was for them "not to lose their control" in difficult situations. There was Tom, the steel company executive who said, "I've learned as a leader that you just can't react viscerally every time something comes up because it just scares people away." And Karen, a food services manager who wanted to "strangle" an employee after discovering that the employee had wrongly accused their company of violating federal health and safety regulations, said that she realized it was "totally inappropriate for me to act annoyed or angry or frustrated because I wasn't going to be able to deal constructively with the problem if I did."

However, while the leaders had learned that they need to remain "composed" in the face of adversity, they also recognized that striving to do so presented a potential trap. If they appeared composed all the time, they could not adequately express empathy and support for others. Sondra, another district manager for the state's child protective services agency, was particularly eloquent about this dilemma. She said, "Sometimes you want to break down and you want to cry. What we hear sometimes is just so *horrific*. . . . I mean, there are some cases that are just really, you know . . . there are just no words." She then talked about the need to control those emotions without losing one's humanity:

> It's not that you're not emotional. You do have to have a certain level of empathy to work with families, so you don't want to lose that; once you lose that, you become a mechanical person and you lose your sense of humanity. But by the same token, you have to balance that because at the end of the day, people are looking to you to take them through the battlefields. So you can't be the one falling and crying in the middle of the field.

Like the other leaders we interviewed, Sondra understood that it was frequently necessary for her to keep in check her own feelings in order to help her staff deal with the crises they often faced. However, she also understood that feelings such as caring and compassion needed to be expressed during these incidents.[7] Too much or too little empathy was not good for her or the organization. While it was necessary to remain open to distressing feelings, the leaders in this study knew not to become overwhelmed by them. By creating a healthy distance, they were in a better position to utilize their emotional and cognitive skills in facing challenges that came their way. Their understanding of how their own feelings affected others made these leaders recognize that they had to balance detachment with concern.[8]

DEFUSING DISRUPTIVE EMOTIONS IN OTHERS BY ACKNOWLEDGING THEIR FEELINGS

There were several other ways in which the leaders used their understanding of how their actions affected others' emotions. Martha had learned that acknowledging the feelings of people with whom one has a conflict can help defuse negative emotions and lead to a satisfactory resolution, as well as better relationships. She used this insight to resolve conflicts with the music director at the church where her support program for children shared space: When the music director would berate Martha with issues of conflict, Martha did not disagree with her; instead, she sympathized with the distress. Martha explained, "It discharges the energy, and she doesn't have to be so defensive and fighting because I'm not resisting." Martha noted that she also agreed with the music director whenever she could. She emphasized, however, that she only did so when she genuinely agreed. Seeking common ground and highlighting it did not mean that Martha stopped focusing on the course of action she considered necessary.[9]

Acknowledging the feelings of others, as well as expressing our own feelings clearly and effectively, can be more difficult when we use email. Many of us have come to rely on email to communicate with others at work, but the leaders in our study were aware that it could sometimes have an undesirable emotional impact. Amy, the nursery school director, found that it was usually unwise to use email when communicating with parents about a sensitive issue. As she put it, "If it's a question about what the curriculum is or what you are doing tomorrow, emails are great. But not when you're talking about a child and you're approaching a difficult subject. The further you get away from personal contact, the more you can have misunderstandings."

SYMBOLS AND ACTIONS CAN BE MORE POWERFUL THAN WORDS

History offers many dramatic examples of how leaders have used symbolic actions to influence others through emotional channels. One of our favorites is the way in which George Washington prevented a mutiny by some of the Continental army's top officers during the American Revolution. The officers were angry because Congress had reneged on its promise to provide back pay and pensions to the troops. After several appeals to Congress were ignored, the officers met in secret to plan a mutiny. Washington heard about the meeting, and "just as the meeting of approximately 500 officers came to order, Washington strode into the hall and asked permission to speak." He began to talk about why the mutiny was unwise. Then he took out a letter from a sympathetic member of Congress and began to read it. After stumbling over a few words, Washington stopped and pulled out a pair of eyeglasses. His men had never seen him wear the glasses before. As he put on the glasses, he said, "Gentlemen, you must pardon me, for I have grown not only gray but blind in the service of my country." According to one report, "The officers were stunned. Many openly wept. Their mutinous mood gave way immediately to affection for their commander." After finishing the letter and saying a few more words about the men's "patient virtue" and the "glorious example you have exhibited to mankind," Washington left the hall. The officers quickly adopted a resolution thanking Washington for his words and pledging faith in Congress.[10]

We do not know whether Washington's use of his eyeglasses was part of a calculated strategy. However, he had never worn the glasses in front of any of his men before, and he took them out to read the letter after his initial remarks failed to sway the disgruntled officers. (It is also interesting that he chose to read a letter from a member of Congress who was sympathetic to the soldiers—an emotionally intelligent move on his part. It may have helped the soldiers reconsider their anger and not feel as though all of Congress was against them.) In any case, the action, which symbolized Washington's own unswerving commitment to the cause, dramatically changed the mood of the group. The mutiny was averted. Six months later the treaty with Britain, ending the war and recognizing the United States as an independent country, was signed.

Many of the leaders in our study also used symbolic actions to influence others. Aaron, for instance, mentioned that he had recently attended the wake for the wife of a long-term employee. It was inconvenient, it took up a considerable amount of time, and he did not have to do it. But Aaron understood how much pride it brought the employee having the leader of the company attend such an event: "He was proud of that. It meant he was important to the company. What a great thing!" Part of what made Aaron such an effective leader is that he understood how these small gestures affected the way people felt about the company. They sent a message to all the employees that this leader, and this company, cared about the people who worked in the trenches.

CONCLUSION

Understanding the causes and effects of emotions is a basic EI ability that people can use in many different ways. One important way in which the leaders in our study used it was to anticipate how their feelings and actions might impact others. It became a strategy they used often and with great effect. Box 3.1 summarizes the leaders' insights about the impact of their feelings on others.

Box 3.1   LEADERS' INSIGHTS ABOUT HOW THEIR FEELINGS AND ACTIONS INFLUENCE OTHERS' EMOTIONS

1. If the leader "loses it," others will as well.
2. A leader's positive feelings can help set a positive tone for a group or larger organizational unit.
3. A leader's openness in expressing his or her feelings will increase others' loyalty and engagement
4. A leader's physical presence during a crisis can help calm others.
5. Getting people to talk more about "good news" will help lift their mood.
6. Symbolic actions can increase others' loyalty and engagement.
7. Agreeing with the other person in a conflict situation can help defuse the negative feelings and facilitate reaching an agreement.
8. Email messages are not a good way to communicate information that might be emotionally charged.
9. People may differ in their emotional reactions to a leader's actions.

ACTIVITY 3.1: BECOMING MORE AWARE OF OUR IMPACT
ON OTHERS

It is often difficult to become more aware of the emotional impact
we have on others. But one way we can do so is by observing the
impact others have on us. The following exercise is designed to help
you become more aware of both the negative and the positive ways
in which another person's behavior affected you.

Instructions

1. Think of a time when you experienced a person's negative influ-
   ence during an interaction.
   - What did the person do or say that felt negative to you?
     (E.g., was it something the person said or didn't say?
     His or her body language? Tone of voice?)
   - What impact did it have? On you? On others?
   - How did you respond?
   - What factors might have influenced the situation?
   - If you could switch places with the person who was the nega-
     tive influence, what would you have done differently?
2. Now think of a time when you experienced a person's positivity
   during an interaction.
   - What did the person do or say that felt positive to you?
   - What impact did it have? On you? On others?
   - How did you respond?
   - What factors might have influenced the situation?
   - If you could switch places with the person who was the positive
     influence, was there anything you would have done differently?

ACTIVITY 3.2: AN EXPERIMENT IN POSITIVITY

This exercise involves conducting a small experiment for yourself. Throughout this chapter we read about leaders like James and

Clarence who knew that staying positive and supportive even in the face of adversity was also the path to keeping others in a positive and productive mindset. Because your emotions are contagious, the goal of this experiment is to see if you can "infect" others with a more positive mood by doing something positive yourself. Of course, you don't need adversity to conduct this experiment. You can practice being more positive in the smallest of ways no matter what the circumstances may be. It also does not require you to become a whole new person! Rather, it is an opportunity to try something new—big or small—that will affect people in a positive way. And don't worry if it doesn't go completely as planned. Just notice what happens, make a mental note, and experiment by trying something else.

Instructions

1. Brainstorm several ideas on how you could set a more positive tone. One way of coming up with ideas is to think about what you would find positive and uplifting if you were to be in somebody else's shoes. Some ideas to get you started might be to greet people differently, tell a humorous story, smile, bring food to share, reassure someone, thank people for their contributions, or make an effort to personally say hello or visit others. Feel free to try one of these or see if you can come up with a few of your own.
2. Pick an idea that feels comfortable and doable for you, and try it out. (Remember it can be a very small gesture.)
3. Record your findings. Be prepared to take notice: How did people respond when you implemented your idea? Notice your own response. Was it difficult or easy to be more positive? Why?
4. If you had to perform the experiment again, what would you do differently?

NOTES

1. Twenty-two of the 25 leaders in the study used this strategy for dealing with a critical incident. Of the 126 incidents described by the leaders during the interviews, 35 involved the use of this strategy.
2. Bryant (2011, January 16).
3. Bryant (2011, June 19).
4. Caruso and Salovey (2004).
5. We describe the classic study by Barsade (2002) in Chapter 2.
6. Cherniss (2006).
7. König, Graf-Vlachy, Bundy, and Little (2018) have proposed that a certain amount of empathy will help leaders to deal with crisis situations, but too much can be detrimental. As they note in their abstract, empathy helps leaders to "recognize warning signs more quickly, have access to more crisis-related information, gain greater stakeholder appreciation via displays of compassion," and be more committed to "healing the organization's relational system." However, too much empathy may cause leaders to be "more predisposed to false alarms, more biased in processing crisis-related information, over-inclined towards apologetic sensegiving, and less committed to repairing the organization's operational system." The outstanding leaders in our study used their emotional intelligence to maintain just the right amount of empathy in any given situation and to vary the amount as the situation required.
8. See Humphrey (2012) for an incisive discussion of how leaders deal with the "emotional labor" that is part of their roles.
9. For more on the emotional aspects of managing conflict, see Shapiro (2016).
10. This account of what came to be known as the "Newburgh Conspiracy" comes from Chernow (2010) and Miller (2010).

4

What Is It Like for Others?

Another way leaders used their emotional intelligence was to put themselves in the shoes of others.[1] This strategy not only helped them to empathize with others but also provided a different perspective on the situation, which often led to better analysis and more effective action.

STRATEGY 4: PUT YOURSELF IN OTHERS' SHOES

As director of a suburban preschool, Amy believes that putting herself in the shoes of parents is imperative when it comes to having difficult conversations with them. She understands that when parents come in to talk about problems involving their young children, they often are anxious and sometimes even angry. And Amy's own anxiety, frustration, and irritation from the school's vantage point can make it especially difficult for her to empathize with the parents in these situations. However, by putting herself in the parents' shoes, she is able to better appreciate their perspective, which helps her to manage her emotions, provide the parents with sympathetic reassurance, and ultimately achieve better outcomes for the child. This helps Amy to understand better not only how they are feeling but also *why* they feel that way. As she put it in our interview, "There's nothing more important to people than their children, so it's very, very hard for them to be objective. Doesn't matter if you're in the right because it's a totally subjective feeling of protecting your child."

One way that Amy put herself in the parents' shoes was to use her own experience as a parent: "I think that I relate to the parents as how I would feel as a parent. . . . I'm a mom. I understand having a young child. I could recall times when the preschool teacher called me about something with my daughter, and the feeling I got. . . . So I'm always asking, 'How might I feel sitting in their situation?'" Amy also uses role playing to gain perspective, especially when preparing for a parent conference about a child's problem. She sets up the role play by asking questions to help her and the teachers better understand the parent's point of view: "I will say to the teacher, 'Let's play this one out. How do you think they are going to respond? What are the possibilities?'" Amy then added, "We're all parents, so we can be sensitive to the fact that we are dropping a bombshell half the time on these people who have not wanted to see that there is an issue."[2]

Many factors make Amy an outstanding leader, but her ability to put herself in others' shoes is particularly important. It has helped her achieve a more nonjudgmental and sensitive frame of mind, which in turn has helped parents, teachers, and other key people in a child's life to understand that there may be something going on with the child that they have not been able or willing to see. The result: Destructive conflict is transformed into constructive problem-solving.[3]

PUTTING ONESELF IN ANOTHER'S SHOES
BY VISITING THEIR WORK SETTING

Sondra, a district manager in a protective services field office, uses a different method:

> In this particular case, we had a child death. It started out as a very
> low-level case—the family needed electricity, so a worker went out
> and looked around. Two weeks later, an infant was found dead in
> the house. What happened was that when the worker went into the
> home, she had never gone down into the basement where there was a
> crib and an additional child. . . . So when the case came up for review,
> people wanted to know why the worker didn't know.

Some supervisors might have come down hard on the worker in this situation. That is certainly how Sondra's bosses, along with elected officials, the media, and the public, might view it. In these kinds of cases, there is a strong tendency to blame the worker, fire the worker, and close the case. However, before the review hearing Sondra decided to visit the home herself to get a better feel for why the worker acted as she did. "And when I saw the home, I realized that it would be very difficult to see that there was a basement." Sondra went on to say:

> When someone's just telling you the story, you think, "Why didn't
> this happen?" But when you actually go into a home, and you see
> some of the dynamics of what the worker might have seen or not
> seen, you understand it a little better. And so I was able to describe
> what happened at the hearing with more empathy—in terms of what
> the worker went through and what they experienced. And they could
> see why a worker might not have gone into the basement.

Putting herself physically into the same setting helped Sondra to better understand how it appeared to the worker, but other supervisors also might have visited the home without changing their opinion about the worker. They might have looked at the location of the basement door and thought, "Well, I can see the basement door quite clearly. Why couldn't the worker see it?" But a more emotionally intelligent view would recognize that it would be easier to notice signs of a basement if you already knew it was there. When Sondra visited the home, she knew there was a basement, but she realized that the worker would not readily notice the basement if she were not looking for it.

Sondra's ability to put herself in the worker's shoes not only helped her and the review board view the worker more sympathetically; it also helped them make a better decision. The way Sondra handled the situation also helped the rest of the workers feel more supported, which contributed to improved staff morale and better relationships between staff and administration. Putting herself in one worker's shoes also provided Sondra with the opportunity to show all her workers that she would go to bat for them.

Research confirms that we are more sympathetic and supportive toward others when we become more aware of their experiences. In one study, the researchers had undergraduates write about something that had happened to them or to someone they knew.[4] The students then were to imagine that they were in charge of a large sports event and had to make several important decisions about it. Finally, the students completed a brief questionnaire that assessed how concerned they were about others in the sports event. The items included "I sometimes think about how my decisions impact others," "I need to take care of others' needs," and "I am concerned about others' well-being." The researchers found that the students who had written about others' experiences before completing the leadership task were more concerned about people involved in the task. The study suggests that when leaders put themselves in the shoes of others, they become more sensitive and caring.

SAVING THE COMPANY FROM A MAJOR MORALE CRISIS

Jonathan, the senior vice president for human resources at a large medical supplies firm, helped his company avoid a costly labor-management conflict by actively taking the perspective of nonmanagement employees. The stage was set when the senior management team established goals and targets for the year: "We set a target for ourselves and communicated a plan to our board and our investors that was way, way, *way* too ambitious. Our bonuses were linked to that plan; and now as the year went on, it became obvious that there was not a snowball's chance we were going to achieve those targets."

As a result of this mistake, none of the employees would receive bonuses at the end of the year. Jonathan realized that such an outcome would have a devastating impact on morale. Relations between top management and workers would suffer because the workers would be paying for a mistake that top management had made.

So Jonathan and other members of the top management team went to the board and said, "Our employees are really busting their humps to achieve respectable results, so we don't want them to be denied a bonus if we fall short of our goals this year. We're the ones who set the goals, not the employees who are working so hard to get the work done." They asked the board to withhold the bonus for top management but grant a small one for the rest of the employees.

All HR professionals should consider employee morale when these compensation issues arise, but not all of them do so. Jonathan's actions stand out not only because he was able to empathize with the employees but because he was able to do so in a situation where he could have been easily distracted or feel pressured to ignore the employees' feelings.

Research confirms that people appreciate their boss's consideration for their needs and feelings. One study looked at what happened when a group of people went through a major organizational change. The researchers found that many of the workers "appreciated when their leaders understood how they felt about the change, and they found that this form of support gave them strength in coping with the emotional demands of change processes and outcomes. As a result, they viewed the change more favorably." For example, when leaders consistently acknowledged their workers' feelings, it reinforced good relationships. While it may or may not have resulted in increased organizational commitment, leaders' acknowledgment of feelings helped the workers come to terms with the negative repercussions and difficult processes associated with the change. Those workers whose feelings were not acknowledged or supported by their boss were more likely to feel a sense of anguish or alienation during the change process. For some, it was the straw that broke the camel's back in their decision to quit the organization. Nevertheless, change in organizations was viewed more favorably by employees when their own emotions were taken into account rather than ignored by their bosses.[5]

WHAT HELPS LEADERS TRULY SEE
THE PERSPECTIVES OF OTHERS?

Putting oneself in others' shoes is a habit of thinking that leaders—even those with a high level of emotional intelligence—often need to learn. Lisa Price, founder and president of Carol's Daughter, a cosmetics firm, talked about how it was hard for her to become an effective leader because initially she didn't put herself in the shoes of others.[6] She said that when she first became a boss, "I had to learn that everyone wasn't like me." For example, while she preferred a high degree of autonomy for herself and worked effectively with it, some of her employees didn't. When she began to impose more limits and direction on those employees, she discovered that they did not mind. In fact, they responded positively. She then realized that much of her concern about being more commanding came from her, not them. As she said, "I just had to accept that I was the one who was the most uncomfortable." It was a hard lesson to learn, but it helped Lisa see the value of putting herself in others' shoes.

Other leaders also learned to put themselves in others' shoes as a result of experiences earlier in their careers. Michael, a president of a billion-dollar global agriculture business, spoke about the strain that conference calls caused for him early in his career when he was living in another country. At the time, he was living in Asia, while the company's headquarters was based in Philadelphia: "Most of our calls were at night Asia time, but people in the home office forgot that fact when I was on the phone."

That early experience helped Michael to be more sensitive to people's time when he became a leader. When building his virtual teams both at home and abroad, he arranges overseas conference calls to take into account time zone changes so that those who have already worked a full day will not be overly burdened with joining the calls.

While changing times for a conference call at first glance might not seem like a big deal, Michael believes "it pays dividends" in building good-will and alignment. Employees get the message that the people in North America, who are running the business, understand and care about the other cultures represented in the business. Timing can be important. Leaders like Michael understand that because remote employees can be even more difficult to connect with on an emotional level, conference calls that are organized at a terribly inconvenient time can easily breed resentment among team members. Remaining sensitive to his own experience of working overseas enabled Michael to pay attention to the seemingly small yet important details of building a successful global business.

When we listened to the leaders talk about how they put themselves in others' shoes, we discovered that they often used four specific techniques, which anyone can use. First, the leaders often called on their own experiences in similar roles and situations, as when Michael remembered the hardships placed by overseas conference calls; and Amy, as director of a nursery school, put herself in the shoes of her parents by thinking about her own experience as a parent. Role playing with her teachers was a second method that Amy used to better anticipate how the parents might be feeling about an upcoming meeting with her. A third technique was in vivo observation, which Sondra used when she visited the home one of her workers had inspected earlier in order to better understand from the worker's perspective why she missed an important clue.

Finally, the leaders often found it easier to see others' points of view by considering their roles, status, and group memberships in the organization. When Diane, a new female employee in charge of leadership training for a large company, proposed that the company consolidate all the leadership training into a single entity, she identified all the stakeholders and then tried to anticipate what their reactions would be. She determined that a particular senior executive, whose support was vital, would not be enthusiastic because of the effect it would have on his power to influence the training his people received. She also understood that going up against someone with so much more clout within the company could be a recipe for disaster. By putting herself in his shoes, she was able to "get inside his head" and consider questions such as "What would be important to him? What kinds of things was he resistant to or passionate about?" She was thus able to develop an empathic understanding of the executive and use it to build a strong case for the new idea. Although he was initially opposed to the proposal and raised many concerns along the way, he eventually supported it. Diane's assessment of his role, status, and group memberships within the company helped her determine what might make him more amenable to the idea.

CONCLUSION

The leaders in our study often used their emotional intelligence to better understand not only how people felt but also *why* they felt the way they did. Whether they were facing an angry parent, a disengaged employee, or an important but reluctant potential donor, the leaders used the strategy of "putting themselves in others' shoes" to better understand why others felt the way they did. This strategy helped increase their empathy, which contributed to better relationships. But it also contributed to better analysis and action.

ACTIVITY 4.1: THE ART OF EXPRESSING EMPATHY

Empathy can be communicated in the smallest of ways, not only in how well we listen but also in what we say and the questions we ask. Yet, often in trying to be empathic, we communicate our own opinion and/ or advice, which can make the recipient feel upset and misunderstood. The art of being empathic as a leader involves communicating a sense of openness and willingness in finding out "why" people feel the way they do—something the leaders in our study were very effective at doing. Sometimes, it is all that is needed for the other person to find the right direction or move beyond an impasse.

The following exercise is one that you can do with another person whom you would enjoy working with and who is willing to experiment with new ideas. The goal of this activity is to practice "putting yourself in another's shoes." It involves you asking and listening to your partner describe an experience and then summarizing what you heard in terms of what his or her experience was like. Remember that you are trying to feel and experience the situation through the other person's eyes—not yours. The following instructions include some key questions and phrases that might be helpful to use during the conversation.

Instructions

1. Ask your partner to describe something that happened at work (or at home) that made him or her feel a particular way.
2. During the conversation, try to focus on what the other person is saying. Use one or more of the following key questions/phrases as prompts to learn more about his or her experience.
   - I wonder what that's like for you.
   - Tell me more.
   - I am interested in hearing what was going on for you when that happened.
   - What do (or did) you think about that?
   - What might an outsider not know about the situation?
   - What's your perspective on that?
   - What else can you tell me?
   - I understand what you're saying.
3. Since the objective is to really pay attention and listen, try to refrain from writing down notes.
4. After the other person has finished describing the experience, reflect back to that person what you heard about why he or she

felt the way he or she did. You can begin by saying, "This is what I heard you saying. Tell me if I am off base in any way."

5. As you are reflecting the story back to your partner, let the conversation flow. Ask the other person to clarify any parts of the story that were misunderstood or incomplete.

6. After it is over, talk about what this experience was like for both of you. (This would be a great time to write down any "aha" moments.)

7. Repeat this exercise two more times with the same person or with someone new.

NOTES

1. Twenty-one of the incidents, involving 15 of the leaders, involved putting themselves in others' shoes.

2. Psychological research has suggested that there are at least two distinct forms of empathy. Cognitive empathy involves the ability to take the perspective of another person. In emotional empathy, one shares the emotional response of others (Davis, 1983; Decety & Jackson, 2004). "Putting oneself in others' shoes" involves both types of empathy, but primarily the cognitive component. As such, it utilizes the ability to understand emotion.

3. As S. E. Murphy (2002) wrote, "Those people who feel that they are truly understood may be more likely to listen to the leader's ideas and implement his or her plans" (p. 175).

4. Scholl, Sassenberg, Scheepers, Ellemers, and de Wit (2017).

5. Smollan and Parry (2011, p. 447).

6. Bryant (2010, August 22).

What Are Those Feelings Telling Us?

Imagine that a manager sits down to meet with an employee who is often late to work in the morning. As she listens to what the employee says, the manager attempts to better understand what is motivating the employee's behavior by tuning into the *emotional dynamics*. Those dynamics may have much to do with the employee's lateness. For instance, the employee may be preoccupied with personal family problems that are competing for his time. Or it may be a matter of values—he works to live, not lives to work. Another possibility is that there are interpersonal conflicts within the work group that are reducing the employee's motivation and commitment. Competing commitments such as family problems, personal values, and interpersonal conflicts are three of the underlying factors that can influence a person's emotions and behavior in the workplace.

We often think of problem-solving as a purely cognitive, analytical process. But what if the underlying dynamics of a problem include an emotional component? Then a person's ability to understand emotions and how they work will be particularly useful in figuring out what is going on. The leaders in our study often used their understanding of emotions to help them uncover the dynamics of a problem or opportunity.[1]

STRATEGY 5: DECIPHER THE UNDERLYING EMOTIONAL

DYNAMICS OF A SITUATION

Researchers David Caruso and Peter Salovey provided a good example of how this strategy can help leaders deal with critical problems.[2] A group of employees at a financial services company had suffered a major drop in productivity and morale after being moved to a new site, away from many of their colleagues. Management tried to address many of the potential causes, such as faulty air conditioning and new processes, to no avail. Finally, an emotionally astute leader determined that the underlying cause had to do with the group's loss of connection with the employees left behind in the old location. Based on this realization, management was able to mitigate the problem, and morale improved along with productivity.

FIGURING OUT HOW TO MANAGE THE "PARENT COMMITTEE"

Several of the leaders in our study also used their understanding of emotions to deal with challenging situations. Amy, the suburban nursery school director, was one of them. She met regularly with a group of parents who made up the "parent committee." At one such meeting, three of the parents said they wanted a year-end "graduation party" for their 4-year-olds. Amy was not enthusiastic about the idea: "We had never done graduation before, and the teachers of the 4-year-olds had thought this was not a good idea because some children might get anxious." The discussion went on for a while and became heated. As Amy put it, "The parents . . . were very emphatic! They suggested that other schools do this, and said, 'I don't see why you can't do this!'" Amy felt "more and more isolated and more and more defensive." She wanted to check with her faculty before making any decisions. However, the parents were relentless. Amy recalled, "I kept getting pushed for an answer, and so it got more and more heated and I got more and more uncomfortable. Eventually I just said to the person who was the head of the committee, 'This really can't be solved today.' And so the meeting ended on a very stressful note." Everyone was still very upset, and no one was satisfied.

After the meeting, the head of the parent group followed Amy out of the room and confronted her in the hallway. "She yelled at me, really yelled at me and said, 'I have never had anyone speak to me the way you spoke to me today. How dare you!'" Fortunately, Amy was able to remain calm at that point, which helped the parent calm down. Amy ended the discussion by saying, "Let's agree to meet again—let's say, by this time next week. I'll try very hard to come up with some way so this doesn't happen again. If you can think of anything, let me know because we obviously both want the same thing." Amy then said to the interviewer, "So we left it in a nice place. I walked out of there feeling that I had done the right thing for the school."

Later, as Amy reflected on what happened, she realized that the structure of the situation contributed to her reaction: When she is the only administrator at a meeting of parents and they make demands, she is likely to become "extremely defensive" and anxious. She explained:

When there are two or three people talking at me at once, it almost feels like bullying—like ganging up. I don't like that format. . . . You can be talking in a constructive way, but it can deteriorate pretty quickly if you get that feeling that there are three or four people that are not being reasonable. You feel like you have to keep answering, and they get defensive, and finally you want to say, "Well forget this!" So I think an administrator, as the person who is in charge, has to be a little cautious about what the format is when they want to address a particular group.

Amy's insight about the emotional dynamics led to several constructive changes in the way she managed future committee meetings. She put into place a modified version of *Robert's Rules of Order*, a guide first published in 1876 for conducting meetings and making decisions in groups. Requiring that a group member make a formal motion and that another "second" the motion before it can be considered for a vote are examples of the rules included in this guide.

Amy also arranged for the head teacher to attend the meetings along with her so that she would not have to face the parent group alone. And she established the rule that the agenda for a meeting had to be given out and discussed with her beforehand so that she would be prepared for issues when they came up.

Amy handled this situation effectively in part because she reflected on her emotional reactions after the initial meeting with the parents, which led to an insight about how a certain type of situation affected her emotions and those of others. Using her ability to empathize, Amy could understand how the parents felt about the issue, which helped her to feel more sympathetic and less angry and judgmental about the parents. However, Amy also could step back and understand her own feelings. Like several other leaders we interviewed, she was aware of her "hot buttons"—situations and behaviors to which she was especially sensitive. And she recognized that the parents were "pushing" one of those buttons during the meeting. She realized that if she is put in a room by herself with a group of parents who are upset about something, her anxiety will cause both her empathy and her effectiveness to deteriorate markedly.

Amy's insights into how the larger cultural context might be contributing to the parents' insistence on this "ceremony" also helped her deal with the situation. She said, "We're dealing with a lot of guilt with parents. There are all these expectations for our children to go to college and so forth. And both parents are working, so they have a lot of stresses and strains." Dealing with parents who are worried about their very young children showing their "achievements" could be frustrating or annoying for Amy and her staff, but the ability to put the parents' behavior in a larger context and see the influence of cultural values helped Amy and her staff manage their own emotions. Specifically, it led to greater empathy, which ultimately contributed to better relationships and outcomes.

HOW UNDERSTANDING THE EMOTIONAL
DYNAMICS SAVED A LEADER'S CAREER

Yolanda, a high-level executive for a large clothing manufacturer, came close to being fired early in her career. What saved her was her ability to step back from the situation and analyze what was happening at the emotional level. The incident began shortly after she joined the company. Her boss asked her to fill in for her at an important meeting while she was out of town. Yolanda did so and thought all had gone well until her boss returned. As Yolanda recalled: "She accused me of 'wanting her job'! She was upset that I had participated at the meeting in a way that looked like I had made a decision or something. . . . It was a very disconcerting kind of conversation. So time went on, and I found myself having difficulty in my relationship with her. It just didn't feel great and it wasn't collaborative. It seemed like we both avoided each other to some degree."

Eventually, Yolanda's boss called her in for a conference. "She sat down with me and said, 'I'm your boss. You better get that. And if you can't adapt, maybe you don't belong here. Are you sure you want to be here?' . . . She also complained that I wasn't responsive to her requests. She had a whole laundry list of things. It was written down, and she was angry."

Yolanda was shaken by the meeting. "Afterward, I was like, 'What hit me?' I was stunned, totally stunned. . . . That had never happened to me in my whole life. I was blown away." After "6 to 8 weeks of depression and struggle," Yolanda realized that she had to make some changes in the way she worked with her boss. "I figured out that I had to shift how I was being with her if I wanted to stay here. And I did want to stay here because I was loving the work, the people, and the place. . . . So I just had to work with her differently somehow."

Yolanda described how she used her ability to perceive and understand emotions to figure out the underlying problem and come up with a strategy. She realized that her boss was "very hard to read" and that, in the absence of clear messages from her boss, Yolanda was filling in and making assumptions based on her own feelings and wishes. The result was misunderstanding, confusion, and growing mistrust. This analysis helped Yolanda see that in order to salvage her job, she had to "find a way to kind of open things up so that I can at least understand what the boss needs and what she wants and what's going on. Because otherwise, I'm just going to make it up, and if I make it up, it may not be accurate, and then I'm cooked. . . . So what I learned to do was to ask more questions in a really respectful way and to try and get what her thinking was." Yolanda's strategy worked. She now gets along better with the boss—so much so that she could now say, "God bless her! I have a huge amount of respect for her now. . . . She's done amazing work here. And actually, on some levels, I really like her." And Yolanda went on to rise up the corporate ladder to a high-level position in the company.

Yolanda was convinced that if she had not discovered why she and her boss could not get along, it would have meant the loss of a job she loved. She also believed that the process of figuring it out helped her immeasurably. She stated, "That experience taught me a lot, and I feel good about the fact that I learned how to work with my boss." Yolanda's experience provides another vivid example of how a leader successfully dealt with a critical challenge by deciphering the underlying emotional dynamics of a situation.

DECIPHERING THE EMOTIONAL DYNAMICS WHEN INTRODUCING CHANGE IN AN ORGANIZATION

While some of the leaders described incidents involving conflicts with individuals, others described how they analyzed the emotional dynamics in order to plan and implement change in large organizations. Bruce, the superintendent of a midsize suburban school district, described a change effort that occurred earlier in his career when he was the principal of the middle school. A new superintendent had come in "with lots

of good ideas, but he was a bull in a China shop." For instance, the superintendent summarily changed the schedule in the elementary schools
after just 2 months on the job, without any input from the principals
or staff. Bruce observed how disruptive the change was and how it
generated high levels of confusion and anger, which adversely affected
the educational process and soured the relationship between the superintendent and his staff.

Bruce knew his school was going to be next. So he suggested that the
superintendent allow him to take charge of the implementation. Bruce
explained that it would be better that way because he had "capital with the
faculty after so many years." Still smarting from the resistance and turmoil
that resulted from the change effort in the elementary schools, the superintendent agreed. Bruce spent the next 3 months using a very different
approach. He gave many presentations to the faculty and solicited input
from them. He also set up groups of teachers who did some research on
the new system, and he established "implementation teams" to see how
the teachers could use the extended time in the classroom. The result was
much more positive than the previous attempt. "It worked out really well.
We didn't have any blowback or angst. . . . And it was really because of
the process—giving people some time, soliciting their opinion." Bruce acknowledged that "not everyone believed it was a good idea," but in the end
"they accepted it."

Bruce's approach was successful because he recognized that if the
change process were poorly designed, it would lead to negative emotional
reactions and active resistance on the part of the teaching staff. Those negative reactions then would adversely affect the way in which many of the
teachers interacted with their students and parents. The students would
feel the tension, become more tense themselves, and begin to act out in
various ways. Ultimately, the result would be poorer performance in the
classroom.

Bruce also was successful because he had a good understanding of how
to design the change process so that the teachers would be more receptive. For instance, he recognized that making just one presentation on the
proposed change, no matter how clear and compelling it might be, is not

enough to generate understanding and commitment by those who are to implement the change. Multiple presentations in multiple venues are often necessary. He also realized that soliciting the input of the teachers would generate stronger emotional commitment.

The trust that Bruce had developed with his staff and the community over time was an important part of the equation, but equally important was the way in which he deciphered how the emotional and organizational dynamics were related.

RECOGNIZING AND WORKING WITH OUR "HOT BUTTONS"

In deciphering the emotional dynamics of different situations, the leaders we studied began to see what "pushed their hot buttons," and they used this insight to help them avoid costly mistakes. Amy demonstrated this ability when she realized that meeting with a group of upset parents, on her own and without any warning or preparation, would make her anxious and defensive in ways that affected her performance adversely.

Charles, the head of a family business, also illustrated how the leaders often became aware of their "hot buttons" over time. After describing a frustrating and costly relationship that he had with a customer, which went on for several years, he said, "I should have trusted my gut on this one." He then went on to say that when he first made the deal with that customer, he "really didn't want to go to the meeting." He went anyway, and he was "really brow-beaten and pressured." He then added, "At the end of the day, I gave them everything they wanted." In retrospect, he realized that he had misgivings about the meeting before he went and that he should have sent someone else instead.

Fortunately, Charles was able to learn from this incident. He described a similar situation that occurred a few years later with another customer. This time, he did send one of his managers to represent the company. "And 3 years later, we are still working with the company on very favorable terms." Like several other leaders, Charles recognized something that pushed his hot buttons by analyzing the emotional dynamics of a crit-ical incident, and he used this knowledge to avoid costly mistakes in the future.

William Ury and his colleagues at the Harvard Program on Negotiation have found that the key in reaching a settlement often is to get beyond each party's initial position and identify the underlying interests.[3] By carefully observing our own emotional reactions as well as those of our opponents, we can often discern more clearly what the important under-lying interests are. And knowing what our hot buttons are can help in this task.

There are a number of ways in which we can come to know what our hot buttons are. In addition to monitoring our physiological reactions, we also can recognize our hot buttons by becoming more aware of how we typically respond. Ury mentions a few of the more common hot but-tons that trip up people: "Some of us react bitterly to even minor criticism or see red when we think someone is making fun of us. Some of us can't stand to have our ideas rejected. Others of us give in because we feel guilty, or because we are worried people won't like us, or because we don't want to cause a scene."[4]

Our hot buttons are a useful guide to our negative emotions. But we also have more positively charged triggers, which can stimulate positive emotion, leading to creative, effective action. When leaders know what their positive triggers are, they can capitalize on potential opportunities by seeking out those situations. Dorothy, for example, discovered early in her career that she enjoyed putting together newsletters. She found both the writing and the graphic design components to be highly enjoyable. So when she became the head of a small community-based organization, she took on the newsletter even though she could have looked for a volunteer to do it. The result was not only a very effective newsletter but also a leader who was more satisfied and engaged because she spent time doing some-thing that was especially rewarding and a little different from her day-to-day responsibilities.[5]

In sum, understanding what their hot buttons were, and using this knowledge when dealing with critical situations, was one of the most important ways in which the outstanding leaders used their emotional intelligence.

UNDERSTANDING THE EMOTIONAL DYNAMICS
OF TAKING ON A NEW LEADERSHIP ROLE

The leaders in our study used their understanding of emotion to analyze the underlying dynamics in many different types of situations. This strategy seemed to be especially vital when they first assumed a leadership role in a group or organization.[6] Harold faced a particularly challenging situation when he became the CEO of a large supermarket chain. He replaced someone who had been the CEO for 30 years and was "something of a legend." Also, it was an old family business, and Harold was the first non–family member to take over the top leadership position.

Replacing a popular leader and respecting the traditions of a company with such a strong culture was a daunting challenge. Harold still remembered his feelings many years later: "When I was sitting there, hearing Bill give this emotional farewell speech to 2,000 people, I was asking myself, 'What am I getting myself into here?' You feel the pressure. You feel the emotion of it. I'll never forget that night." At one point in his speech, the outgoing CEO said, "Don't worry, if things don't go well after I leave, I'll be on the next plane back from Florida!" Although it was meant as a joke and got a good laugh, it reflected the anxiety and ambivalence that the outgoing CEO, along with many others in the company, had about his retiring. It also did not help that newspapers at the time ran stories about the change in leadership and referred to Harold as "the outsider." Even worse was the skepticism of people within the company. Harold said, "A lot of people didn't think I'd be able to do it. They thought I'd only last a couple of years because I was an outsider and was replacing such a strong leader."

Rather than fall apart in the face of such pressure or try to ignore it, Harold used these insights about the underlying emotional dynamics to plan his transition into the leadership role. His basic strategy was to find an approach that was consistent with his style but also compatible with the company's traditions and values. And Harold succeeded. The company flourished under his leadership, and when he chose to retire after almost a decade, he was admired and respected by both the employees and the board of directors.

Looking back, Harold said, "What I did here is not something that was taken out of a textbook. It was something that was culturally appropriate in a company that values the culture more than anything else." Harold's habit of deciphering the emotional dynamics of a situation continued to guide him through the many challenges that he faced as the head of a large company during a turbulent period. The key lesson: Whenever a leader assumes a new position, there are emotional dynamics that will affect how others react to him or her, and deciphering what those are can help the leader better navigate this important transition.

CONCLUSION: UNDERSTANDING THE EMOTIONAL DYNAMICS AT MULTIPLE LEVELS

What was especially striking about all these stories was that the leaders understood how factors at multiple levels influenced people's emotions. For instance, at the *societal* level, Amy understood that some parents were "difficult" because of the pressure created by cultural values and expectations. Bruce's efforts to implement a scheduling change in his school illustrated an understanding of how dynamics at the *group and organizational* levels affect emotions. Yolanda's difficulties with her boss ultimately required that she understand the way in which *interpersonal* dynamics—specifically, their contrasting communication styles—contributed to the problem. The conflict between Amy and some members of the parent committee was resolved in part because she was able to step back and recognize how her own anxiety made her more defensive, which made the parents even more upset—an example of emotion understanding at the *individual* level. Important emotional dynamics occur at all these levels, and understanding the contribution of each level is another way in which outstanding leaders use their emotional intelligence.

Thus, the leaders in our study were skillful in identifying the causes and effects of emotions, and they used that ability to decipher and deal with the emotional dimensions of challenging situations. They also used it to identify opportunities that were not immediately obvious to others. Doing so became a strategy that they used frequently as they sought to build better relationships with others and accomplish ambitious goals.

ACTIVITY 5.1: UNDERSTANDING OUR EMOTIONAL TRIGGERS

In this chapter, we have read about situations and behaviors to which the leaders were emotionally reactive. We learned that while some "hot buttons" could lead them toward losing a sense of control, other more positively charged triggers enhanced their sense of well-being and their performance as leaders. Effective leaders like Amy and Harold, for example, were able to keep their calm and focus to deal with organizational challenges because they had learned to recognize those emotional triggers that could have easily impaired their performance. Leaders like Dorothy, by growing attuned to a positive trigger connected with a love for writing, discovered a renewed sense of purpose and motivation in creating an effective company newsletter.

The following exercise consists of two parts. While both parts are aimed at developing a deeper understanding of what triggers our emotional reactions, the first part addresses our "hot buttons," and the second part looks at our positive triggers. Feel free to complete both parts, or focus on the one that you feel is particularly relevant. In Chapters 6 and 7, we will discuss the ways in which we can work with these emotional triggers so that there is more freedom and choice in responding in any given situation. So grab something to write with or your laptop, and let's begin!

Part 1

First, write down a description of a time when you had a "hot button" reaction that made you feel frustrated, angry, or sad. (Follow the four Ws—Who was involved? What were you doing? When did it happen? Where did it happen?) Then answer the following questions:

- What were the triggers for this experience? In other words, what was it about the experience that really set you off? (For example, was it something a person said? If so, was it the way he or she said it? Or who the person was? Or how, when, or where it happened?)
- Why do you think these triggers created such a strong emotional reaction?
- What were the specific emotions that got triggered by this hot button? Did those emotions change over the course of the experience? If so, in what ways?
- What, if any, were the consequences of having your hot button pushed? How might it have affected your behavior? Others' behavior? How might it have affected your goals and your ability to accomplish them?

Part 2

As we saw in Dorothy's example, positive emotional triggers can provide vivid clues as to what makes us feel good and what energizes us in ways that improve our performance. Briefly describe one of those times (follow the four W's from Part 1—wo, what, when, where) and then answer the following questions:

- What was the trigger or set of triggers for this experience? What was it about the experience that made you feel good?
- Why do you think these triggers created such a positive emotional reaction?
- What were the specific emotions that got triggered?
- What, if any, were the consequences of having your positive trigger pushed? In what way(s) did it affect your life inside and outside of work?

- How often would you say you experience these positive moments in your life?
- If you haven't experienced these kinds of emotions for a while, why do you think that is?

If possible, share your answers with someone you trust. This will give you even more insight and perspective on how to recognize your emotional triggers. Remember that this exercise is meant to increase your emotional awareness and understanding by helping pinpoint your positive and negative triggers and how having those triggers pushed ultimately affects us. We will talk about how to manage these emotional triggers in the next chapter.

NOTES

1. Eighteen leaders in 28 incidents in our study used their understanding of emotions to decipher the underlying dynamics of a challenge or opportunity.
2. Caruso and Salovey (2004, p. 27).
3. Ury (1991, p. 18). For an update on the work of the Harvard Program on Negotiation, see Shapiro (2016).
4. Ury (1991, p. 26). See also Shapiro (2016).
5. A long-term study of professionals who had recovered from early-career burnout found that "creating a special interest" in the job was a way in which they became more engaged and effective at work (Cherniss, 1995). Dorothy's newsletter was an example. In Chapter 11 we say more about how organizations and leaders can use these "special interests" or personal projects to encourage more emotionally intelligent behavior.
6. There has been some interest in the topics of "leadership succession" and "becoming a leader" among some management theorists. See, for example, Bennis and Nanus (2003); Friedman (1987).

6

Change Perspective

We began this book with the story of Tom, who, as a young manager in his second week on the job, had to face a group of angry engineers from an automobile company that bought steel from Tom's company. They wanted to meet with Tom and his team because Tom's company was one of their worst suppliers. When we asked him how he felt when he received this damning criticism, he said, "I had been in the job literally a week. So part of it was, 'Oh my God, what the hell am I going to do?'"

We saw how Tom not only managed to keep his cool and handle the meeting with the engineers effectively, but continued to do so the next day when he met with his team to discuss the criticism and what they needed to do about it. And within a year, Tom's company had moved from one of the worst to one of the best suppliers for that customer.

When we asked Tom how he managed to control his emotions and keep them from interfering with his judgment, he said that it had to do with his attitude about problems in general and the way he thought about challenging situations. He said, "Businesses are never perfect. There are always challenges and bad news. . . . Nine out of 10 people who walk through my door have a problem. And it is usually too simple to think that all the problems are due to one person screwing up, or that his screwing up is simply caused by incompetence or negligence. The world is usually just more complicated than that." Tom's realistic expectations about his role as a leader helped him to manage his emotions and the emotions of others.

Tom also tried to focus his attention on the task at hand and on fixing the problem, rather than blaming others. When describing his meeting with his team the next day, he said, "My focus was not on beating anyone up, but rather, 'What can we do to fix this?'"

Interestingly, Tom thought his attitude about problems came in part from his training and experience as an engineer. "Engineers," he said, "are used to dealing with problems. That's what engineering is all about." The only thing that changed when he became a manager was the nature of the problems. We do not usually think of an engineering background as helping people to be more sensitive, supportive leaders. However, that background can serve them well if they can apply the problem-solving perspective of the engineer to the motivational and relationship problems encountered by managers. But one does not have to be trained as an engineer to view the world as messy or to recognize that the leader is the one to whom people turn when they have complicated problems they cannot solve on their own.

The way in which one thinks about people and situations affects the way in which one manages emotions. How Tom thought about or "framed" problems helped him modulate the amount of stress that he experienced when confronted with a problem. And his approach shows how reframing the way they think about situations can be a useful emotion-management strategy for leaders.

Richard Lazarus and his colleagues have identified many different ways in which people cope with stress and negative affect.[1] Their research, which spanned several decades, indicated that some ways of coping are more effective than others. In general, "positive reappraisal" (which would include reframing) and "planful problem-solving" are the two approaches that have been most highly correlated with successful adaptation in life. "Suppression of emotion" was one of the least effective, and sometimes it was harmful. Lazarus's earlier research was confirmed by a more recent study, which followed a group of students during their 4 years of college. The researchers found that those who used positive reappraisal more often had stronger social connections and higher social status at the end of the study. On the other hand, those who relied more on suppressing their emotions had weaker social connections.[2]

STRATEGY 6: REFRAME HOW YOU THINK
ABOUT THE SITUATION

We found that the leaders in our study reframed the way they thought about situations in five different ways. First, like Tom, they expected the world to be *complicated and messy*. Second, rather than *playing the blame game*, they looked at factors in the situation that might be causing, triggering, exacerbating, or maintaining a problem. A third way in which they reframed situations was to adopt an *inquiring mindset*. Fourth, they often would manage their emotions and those of others by *focusing on the task* at hand. And fifth, they would try to adopt a more *positive perspective* when confronted with particularly challenging situations.

EXPECT THE WORLD TO BE COMPLICATED AND MESSY

Many of the leaders in our study, like Tom, believed that problems are inevitable and that dealing with the most challenging problems was a major part of their job as organizational leaders. Although they did not think of this outlook as a strategy for managing emotions, we realized that they used it that way repeatedly.[3]

Conflicts will occur in organizations no matter what one does. As Sam, the CEO of a large residential facility for people with disabilities, put it, "You're never going to get complete agreement because people are different and have different opinions." Recognizing that conflicts are inevitable in the messy, complicated world in which we live seemed to help many of the leaders we interviewed to manage their emotions better when faced with such conflicts.

Aaron, the head of a large construction firm, used a baseball analogy to help him realize that his job would often involve problems that he could not fix. He said, "You don't need to get a hit every day. You're not going to get every one of them right. We make mistakes."

For the leaders who worked in agencies charged with protecting children from abuse and neglect, reminding themselves that the "world is messy" proved to be especially helpful for managing their emotions during highly upsetting events. Clarence, after describing the case in which a young child died even though his staff had been monitoring it (see Chapter 3), said, "How do we continue to heal and continue to provide good service, even though we went through that?" Part of the answer for Clarence was to recognize that he and his staff could not do any more than they did to prevent that incident. He said, "There's nothing we could have done to stop that from happening. We can't be in people's lives 24/7 . . . we can't control everything." He reminded himself that the review board determined it was "an unfortunate incident" and that "the case practice was good . . . the staff did their job."

Clarence's belief that he and his staff could not do any more than they did because they "couldn't control everything" could lead to passive resignation and the acceptance of bad situations that might be ameliorated. However, Clarence avoided using reframing as an excuse for inaction. He said that even though they cannot always prevent horrible incidents like the one he had described, he and his staff can work to minimize the frequency of such incidents. Finding ways to do so is what "gives you a sense of accomplishment." Clarence and his staff will fail sometimes because the world is imperfect, but that does not mean they cannot do good work and strive to do even better in the future.

Expectations play a critical role in shaping our emotional responses to situations. When our expectations are unrealistically positive, we are more likely to be disappointed. For leaders, such disappointment can be toxic. If leaders fail to adopt the attitude that the world is inherently messy, they tend to become perfectionistic. They micromanage others, which leads to stress, burnout, anxiety, and discouragement. The emotional turmoil makes it difficult for them to keep things in perspective; they lose sight of the larger picture as they become too caught up in the details. Thus, expecting the world to be complicated and messy often helps leaders to manage their emotions and those of others in ways that enable them to achieve their goals. The old saying "Hope for the best but prepare for the worst" turns out to be a good way to manage our emotions.

DON'T PLAY THE BLAME GAME: LOOK AT ALL THE FACTORS CONTRIBUTING TO THE SITUATION

When things go wrong, we often tend to blame a person or group of people—sometimes others, and sometimes ourselves. Yet, it is usually overly simplistic to think that it is one person's fault. Also, doing so tends to increase emotional reactions such as anger, guilt, and shame, which reduce our ability to come up with effective solutions to problems. Some of the leaders we studied used a reframe that helped them avoid such simplistic and destructive thinking: Rather than blame individuals, they focused on ways in which the situation contributed to what was happening.

Ronald, the principal of a parochial school, described how he managed his feelings by focusing on the situation, rather than play the blame game, when he became embroiled in a conflict with his chief financial officer, an older volunteer who had had a successful career as an accountant in industry. The volunteer was upset with the way in which Ronald had handled the payroll when the volunteer was away on vacation. Ronald believed that there was nothing wrong with how he had handled the payroll and that the volunteer's approach was unnecessarily complicated for a small parochial school. When they met to talk about the situation, Ronald began to feel upset with the "insulting" way the volunteer spoke to him. We asked Ronald how he dealt with his feelings in this situation, and he replied:

> You just need to have an attitude adjustment. So I just stepped back and looked at him and thought how it wasn't him that was frustrating and insulting me, it was the situation. . . . Our school is just not comparable to what he's been used to, which is a much larger operation. . . . So I just focused on the fact that it was no fault of his. And even though he was quite insulting, I didn't take it like it was coming from him. It was just because I was hitting this raw nerve.

Ronald then used an analogy to describe how he tries to avoid blaming either himself or another person when faced with a frustrating situation. He said, "If you're out in the rain, and the car breaks down, it's frustrating. But you don't blame anyone. It's no one's fault. You're just stuck in the situation."

Avoiding the "blame game" worked for Ronald in this situation. He believed that he was able to speak with the volunteer "respectfully" throughout their meeting; in the end, the volunteer agreed to change his role and let someone else monitor the accounts day-to-day, which Ronald thought was the ideal solution.

Some of us tend to blame ourselves when things do not go well; we internalize the blame. Others tend to be externalizers who more often blame others. In either case, we overlook the contribution of situational factors.[4] However, whether we blame ourselves or others, the result usually is anger, guilt, shame, or some other strong negative emotion. Recognizing that there are situational factors contributing to the problem helps us avoid the blame game, which reduces disruptive emotional responses.[5]

ADOPT AN INQUIRING MINDSET TOWARD
THE EMOTIONS DISPLAYED

Like all the leaders we studied, Martha sometimes had to deal with difficult emotions in her job as executive director of a nonprofit agency. After
talking about conflicts that she and her staff have had with the church
where their program is housed, Martha reflected on how she has learned
to be less reactive by turning her reactions into questions: "For me, it's
just learning not to be reactive. Like when someone says something that
pushes a button, sitting back and asking myself, 'OK, what is in play here?
What are their emotions and feelings that are making them behave that
way, and what's going on in me, what am I triggering in them? Am I doing
something I'm not even aware of that's making them react to me in that
way?' "

By adopting an "inquiring mindset,"[6] Martha became aware that she
was having a strong emotional response to the conflicts with the church.
She then was able to step back and reflect on why she and others were
acting as they were. As a result, she shifted from feeling upset, angry, or
anxious to feeling curious.[7]

Adopting an inquiring mindset also can help us use other reframes. It
helps us to appreciate just how complicated and messy the world is, and
switching from a "judging" mindset to an inquiring one can help us avoid
the blame game.[8] Karen, a corporate food services manager, adopted an
inquiring mindset when she met with an employee who had falsely accused her company of violating occupational health and safety regulations.
Karen said that she had wanted to "strangle" the employee when she found
out what the employee had done, but she knew that she had to manage
her emotions carefully in order to resolve the situation effectively and humanely. She did so by approaching the meeting as more of a fact-finding
session than a disciplinary one. Her goal was to better understand why the
employee had acted as she did.

Karen's first step was to reach out to the employee's boss, who told
Karen that the employee had been acting erratically in the last several weeks, getting agitated by minor things and not understanding or

following common instructions. Based on this information, Karen then set up a meeting between herself and the employee. Upon first meeting, Karen noticed that the employee's demeanor was quite different in that she seemed "hesitant to talk and red in the face." With a gentle and open manner facilitated by her desire to learn more about the employee's situation at work and elsewhere, Karen opened up the conversation by asking, "Are you ready for the holidays?," which resulted in the employee going ballistic.

> She literally started screaming at me that she couldn't take off the holiday this year and didn't I understand that? And I said, 'No, I don't understand, but holidays are tough for many people.' And then she completely broke down crying and indicated that her husband had just been diagnosed with cancer and she couldn't understand why this was happening to them. They had lived a good life and they just worked every day to try and get by. And you know, couldn't this happen to somebody who was more deserving of bad luck?

The conversation eventually led to the discovery that the employee's anger was really about the way her husband had been treated by the health care system after receiving a cancer diagnosis. In Karen's assessment, the employee "was just angry with life" and had probably used the complaint as an outlet for her anger. Adopting an inquiring mindset helped Karen not only to manage her own emotions but to help the employee better manage hers as well. Talking further about her husband's condition and directing her toward helpful resources, Karen was able to lead the employee down a more constructive road. In the end, Karen was able to turn the employee from feeling rage and bitterness to feeling cared for and supported. Several months later, the employee was back on the job and acting like her old self.

Most professionals and managers learn to adopt an inquiring mindset toward the more task-related aspects of their work. However, they usually do not learn to use the inquiring mindset to deal with the emotional aspects. Our leaders did so and discovered that it can be another useful way to manage feelings.

FOCUS ON YOUR GOALS AND THE TASK AT HAND

As we went over the dozens of critical incidents that the leaders described, we were moved by the emotional intensity of many. The leaders often described situations in which they had to face great loss, sorrow, frustration, and even hopelessness. When we looked at the ways in which they coped with these feelings, one that came up repeatedly was focusing on the goals and the task at hand while pushing all other thoughts aside.[9]

When Aaron, the CEO of the large construction company, described the sudden death of his mentor, the company's chairman (see Chapter 2), he said, "It was the first time in 32 years I didn't want to come into work." But he knew that the rest of the employees were depending on him more than ever. So he got up and went into work. Focusing on the most important task was a key reframe that Aaron used to manage his feelings after his loss.

Daniel Goleman has noted that when a person is distressed, focusing on something other than the cause of the distress can serve as a helpful distraction. In fact, distraction—the ability to focus one's attention away from disturbing thoughts—is one of the most basic emotional self-regulation skills that we develop as young children. It allows the arousal center of the brain to calm, which frees up more cognitive resources for problem-solving and creative thought.[10] For the leaders in our study, focusing on the goals and tasks at hand served as a particularly effective distraction.

For Doreen, one of the most difficult challenges of her career was helping her students and staff following the terrorist attacks in New York City on 9/11. At that time she was the principal of an elementary school located right across the river in New Jersey. From some windows, they could see the smoke rising from the World Trade Center towers in the distance. Many of the children had parents who worked in downtown Manhattan. According to Doreen, what helped her to "keep it together" during that day and the days that followed was focusing on the goal of "doing what is best for the children, teachers, and parents." Her focus on doing what was best for everyone in her school helped them to manage their distress.

Focusing on the goals and tasks at hand often helps leaders manage the emotions of others as well as their own. As Goleman noted: "A leader's field of attention—that is, the particular issues and goals she focuses on—guides the attention of those who follow her whether or not the leader explicitly articulates it. People make their choice about where to focus based on their perception of what matters to leaders. The ripple effect gives leaders an extra load of responsibility: They are guiding not just their own attention but to a large extent, everyone else's."[11]

Focusing on goals and tasks may work best when they are clearly linked to important, transcendent values. When the goals involve supporting those who depend on the leader, or saving an organization to which one has dedicated oneself for more than 30 years, or creating a better world for one's children and grandchildren, focusing on what we have to do can be an effective strategy for managing our emotions.[12]

Much of what is written about coping with life's demands emphasizes what people can do to take care of themselves. We are told that we should exercise more, change our diets, take up yoga or meditation, and change the way we think about adversity. When it comes to job-related stress, we are even counseled not to focus too much on our work and its demands because too much dedication and commitment can lead to burnout.[13] Thus, it was striking to see how these exceptional leaders often found it helpful to focus on how to take care of others and the larger organization. Sometimes, focusing on the job at hand and why it is important may be a better strategy for managing our emotions than just focusing on ourselves.

ADOPT A MORE POSITIVE PERSPECTIVE

Harold became the CEO of a large supermarket chain just as the Great Recession of 2008 hit the country. Many people in his position would probably think of the situation as bleak. Others might just shrug and hunker down. But Harold actually reframed it as a blessing in disguise. It provided an opportunity for him and his top executives to rethink a plan that had generated much resistance and probably needed more work before it was ready to be implemented. Thus, rather than think of the recession only as something that would put added pressure on everybody, Harold thought of it as something that would actually reduce the pressure in some ways.[14]

"Positive thinking" has been one of the oldest and most popular strategies that people have used to manage their emotions. Even before modern psychology provided scientific evidence that optimism is associated with better health and success,[15] philosophers, religious leaders, and business experts promoted positive thinking. In the first century, the philosopher Epictetus famously said, "The thing that upsets people is not so much what happens, but what they think about what happens."[16] In 1913, a popular novel called *Pollyanna* introduced a technique called "the Glad Game," which involved thinking about something positive whenever one encounters a disappointment or calamity.[17] And in 1952, the clergyman Norman Vincent Peale published a highly popular and influential book with the title *The Power of Positive Thinking*.

Research on leadership suggests that positive reframes can help leaders manage emotions in ways that lead to more positive results. Pescosolido, in a field study of informal leaders in groups such as rowing crews and jazz ensembles, found several instances in which leaders helped their team manage potentially disruptive emotions by using a positive reframe.[18] In one case, a rowing crew had expected to win a race but instead finished close to last. The group was very demoralized right after the race, but their leader shifted the tone:

> Suddenly, Jackie began to cry out loudly and excitedly, exclaiming that the crew had beaten its local rivals, the team that it often lost to in scrimmage races. The women's spirits took an immediate upturn as they all began cheering because they had beaten their local rivals. Several of the members of this crew later described this experience as the best thing that occurred to them during their spring season, suggesting that it gave them confidence, resilience, and the realization that bringing home medals was not the only reason that they participated in the sport.[19]

But what are leaders to do if they are not "naturally" optimistic? Positive thinking seems to be a core part of one's character. We seem to be hard-wired to be either more or less optimistic.[20] Fortunately, psychologists have discovered that there are ways for people to adopt a more positive perspective in certain situations even if they do not have a naturally optimistic temperament.[21] And some of the leaders we studied, like Cynthia, showed how one can do so.

Cynthia did not seem to be a particularly upbeat kind of person. However, she was able to learn how to adopt a more positive perspective on giving and receiving feedback in a leadership development workshop. Initially, Cynthia and many of the other participants talked about how it felt bad to give negative feedback to someone who was doing something wrong. "For most of us," she said, "it feels like going to battle!" As a result, they often "put it off as long as possible." However, the workshop participants came up with a more positive way of thinking about feedback, which is that "it is a gift," something given to the other person to help that person manage his or her roles better. As Cynthia put it, "Even if the feedback is negative, most likely you'll see some nuggets in there to use. So if you reframe your mindset, it reframes your emotion about it."

Because Cynthia was not naturally optimistic, it was somewhat awkward at first for her to use this positive way of thinking about giving feedback. However, she found it easier to do so after seeing how well it worked. She showed how one can learn how to deal with a specific type of emotional challenge by adopting a more positive way of thinking about it, without having to develop a more optimistic temperament.

A number of researchers have described other simple techniques that leaders can use to help them adopt a more positive focus. Judith T. Moskowitz, a professor at Northwestern University, has identified eight "skills to help people foster positive emotions."[22] They include "recognize a positive event each day," "list a personal strength and note how you used it," and "recognize and practice small acts of kindness daily." She and her colleagues have done a number of studies in which they taught people these skills, and the results have been promising. In one such study, they found that people who went through a 5-week online training program reported more positive affect and lower stress levels.[23]

In addition to Moskowitz's work, Caruso and Salovey presented a list of positive self-statements that anyone can use to raise their mood quickly, such as "I am feeling really good today" and "Things are looking up."[24] And Boyatzis and McKee described how a highly effective leader they knew set aside time on a regular basis to read appreciative letters from customers. She would then write notes to her employees who were mentioned in the letters.[25]

Several of the leaders in our study found it especially useful to adopt a more positive view of *other people*. For example, Ronald, the parochial school principal, got upset when he heard that a prominent person in his community had told others not to give any more money to his school. But he could not afford to stay upset because this was someone with whom he needed to maintain a positive, ongoing relationship. So Ronald consciously tried to focus on the good qualities of the person: "I gave myself a mental image of the person. He's a very likable person, and he seems to be a very goodhearted person, so that, itself, had an impact of naturally making me feel sympathetic toward him, looking at him as a person rather than as an adversary or someone who's for some reason working against me."

Interpersonal relations are influenced by one's attitudes toward that person. If we believe that the other person is bad, we will tend to notice and focus on those aspects of his or her character and behavior that tend to conform to this view. Conversely, if we view the other person as basically good, we will tend to notice those aspects that fit with our view, ignoring or minimizing evidence to the contrary.[26] And these perceptions strongly influence how we feel about other people and the quality of our relationships with them.[27]

POSITIVE REFRAMING NEEDS TO BE USED JUDICIOUSLY

In general, viewing people more positively can be helpful in managing emotions. But some employees are capable of doing some really bad things (e.g., Ponzi schemes, insider trading, bribery, sexual harassment). Leaders need to confront them directly, and not only because it is the right thing to do. If they fail to recognize the faults of these offenders and do not take appropriate action, leaders could be exposing their organizations to huge liabilities.

Also, trying to be positive about a situation when it does not fit the context can backfire. For instance, telling those we supervise that things are not so bad during a difficult period, and that all they need to do is try to relax and work hard, may not help them manage their emotions more effectively, especially if they think, "It's easy for him to say. He's in management, and they have it much easier than we do." Even giving ourselves a positive pep talk can be detrimental if it prevents us from tuning in to negative emotions that could provide valuable information about a difficult situation.

Emotionally intelligent leaders acknowledge the downside of a bad situation—the frustrations, the losses, the injustices—and they do not try to minimize it. They recognize that people often need time to vent, to rage, or to mourn. However, these leaders seem attuned to when there has been enough acknowledgment and sharing of the pain, and when it is time for them and others to move on and adopt a more positive outlook.

Outstanding leaders also understand that group norms sometimes make it better not to focus so much on the positive. The leader of the rowing team who enthusiastically pointed to the positive aspects after a disappointing loss later confided to Pescosolido that she would never have done this in her former crew, where the norms for expression of emotion were very different:

> The boat that I was on in high school . . . we were very uptight, very focused. We never would have let on that we were upset by coming in sixth, we would have just all decided individually that we had to work harder, or that we were worthless, or whatever. This group though, we always are talking about everything, about how we feel about everything that happens to us as a group. So when I saw [our local rivals] behind us, and I got excited that we had beat them,

I knew that the others . . . would be excited about it too! But I never would have been able to cheer like that for sixth place in my old boat . . . they would have been all like, 'yeah, but we still blew it."[28]

Contemporary psychological researchers now tend to endorse a more nuanced and balanced view of positive thinking. For instance, Martin Seligman, one of the founders of the positive psychology movement, has noted that there are times when it is better to be pessimistic. He wrote, "The balance of the evidence suggests that in some situations negative thinking leads to more accuracy. Where accuracy is tied to potentially catastrophic outcomes (for example, when an airplane pilot is deciding whether to de-ice the wings of her airplane), we should all be pessimists."[29] Rather than view positive thinking as a panacea, Seligman advocates that we find the "optimal balance between positive and negative thinking."[30]

CONCLUSION: AN OUNCE OF PREVENTION . . .

In using reframing as a strategy for managing emotions, it is sometimes best to reframe challenges or opportunities *before* they occur. In most of the examples that we uncovered, the leaders described how they used reframing to help them manage situations as they unfolded; however, we also heard about ways in which the leaders anticipated a stressful situation or a positive opportunity and used reframing in a more proactive way. For example, we saw earlier how the leaders in Cynthia's company began using a more positive way of thinking about feedback before they sat down for a scheduled feedback meeting with their boss or an employee. When it comes to reframing, "an ounce of prevention" really does seem to be worth a "pound of cure."

In sum, changing the way we think about situations by using the reframes described in this chapter provides effective ways of managing emotions because cognition and emotion overlap. There is a back-and-forth movement between thoughts and feelings that is never static. Emotionally intelligent leaders seem to understand this idea and use reframing as a strategy to manage their emotions and those of others. However, the leaders we studied did not just manage their emotions by reframing how they thought about a situation. They also developed a strategy for modifying situations so that positive emotions naturally arose. We consider this strategy in the next chapter.

ACTIVITY 6.1: ACCENTUATING THE POSITIVE

As you read in this chapter, leaders who adopt the mindset that "life is messy" tend to fare better under pressure, in part because they don't lose sight of the things that are going well. When you're under pressure and trying to navigate your way through a maze of problems, it can be difficult to notice the positive things that happen in your life. However, these are the very times when you most need to do so: Noticing the positive things does more than help us cope with stressful circumstances by improving the way we feel; those positive feelings trigger a cascade of reactions that help us mobilize resources and support and widen our focus for coming up with creative alternatives to problems. This exercise is designed to help you recognize and track those positive events, big and small, that happen every day but often go unnoticed.

Instructions

1. Remember a moment this past week when something positive happened (it can be as simple as getting a phone call from a friend, drinking a cup of coffee, or watching a funny movie).
2. Make a note in as much detail as you would like about the feelings, thoughts, and physical sensations that you experienced at the time.
3. Is there something from that experience that you can build into your life now? What would it be?
4. Make a daily practice of this exercise by noticing and jotting down one or more positive things. This would be a great opportunity to start a journal. Not only will you get better at doing it, but you will feel better as well!

ACTIVITY 6.2: KEEPING YOUR FOCUS ON THE GOAL

Leaders face all kinds of intense situations, some of which can be emotionally destabilizing. Yet outstanding leaders like Aaron, whose CEO and beloved mentor died suddenly of a heart attack at a company conference one morning, have learned to focus on important goals and tasks as a way of coping with intense feelings, without being overwhelmed by them. As you have discovered in this chapter, focusing on goals and tasks allows time for a leader to regroup and move forward by providing a much-needed distraction from the distress caused by upsetting situations. Learning to use this type of reframe, however, does not need to be left to chance. Although it is impossible to predict when the next wave of turbulence may occur, reflecting and learning from our experiences can be a powerful teacher—so that when the inevitable strikes and we are again confronting an emotionally challenging time, we can do so from a place of centeredness and focus.

Instructions

Try to think of an event from your own life when you got sidetracked because your emotions got the best of you. Perhaps you got so frustrated or annoyed that you lost your temper in a meeting. Or you became discouraged and stopped caring about the outcome of a project that once meant a great deal to you. Or maybe you felt overly stressed in trying to reach a deadline. The examples are endless, but pick one for this activity.

1. Rewind in your head to the beginning of the event before you started to feel upset.
2. Now try to remember what you were trying to accomplish before the situation unfolded.
3. Write this down on paper or type in the notes section of your smartphone or laptop.
4. Read it once or twice.

5. Now replay the incident again in your head, but this time don't give in to your unsettled emotions. Instead, stay focused on the goals you have written down.

6. Now think about how the situation might play out. What things do you see yourself doing differently? What basic steps might you see yourself taking to stay on target with your goal?

Over the next week, look for at least one opportunity, inside or outside work, to practice focusing on your goals when things get challenging. Write down in a few sentences what goals/tasks will be important for you to keep in mind during this time. Look at these goals that you have written down at least once a day and reflect on what small step(s) you can take to take to stay on task.

ACTIVITY 6.3: ADOPTING AN INQUIRING MINDSET BY ASKING OURSELVES EMOTIONALLY INTELLIGENT QUESTIONS

It is said that asking good questions "invigorates thinking, learning, action and results."[31] Asking good questions also helps us to adopt an inquiring mindset, which, as you read in this chapter, is a good way to manage our emotions and those of others in challenging situations. We saw how leaders like Tom and Karen adopted an inquiring mindset and used effective questioning skills to handle tough situations that could have easily blown up into major disasters. Without good questions, leaders are more prone to jumping to conclusions, making quick judgments or rash decisions, and ultimately hurting themselves and the people they depend on.

Asking good questions requires us to use our emotional intelligence because our emotions, our biases, and our intentions are often signaled to the receiver in the kinds of questions we ask, whether we know it or not. So, before we can ask good questions of others, we first need to begin by asking ourselves important questions, some of which are outlined in the following.

Instructions

1. Think of a current problem or situation in your work or personal life that feels emotionally charged.
2. Write down what you think is going on. (Don't edit yourself here, just write what comes to mind first.)
3. In thinking about the other person(s) involved, ask yourself, "What may be causing them to feel and behave that way?" What have you observed that might lend support to your conclusions?
4. Then ask yourself these questions: "Could I be doing something that triggers something in them? Or could I be doing something I'm not even aware of that's making them react to me in that way?" If yes, what?
5. How might the situation be contributing to the problem? What other factors might be affecting the situation besides the person?

You might find this exercise a bit challenging, particularly if your situation has a long and problematic history. Remember that the goal of this exercise is to help you adopt an inquiring mindset when faced with a challenging situation and to broaden your emotional awareness and understanding of the situation by considering different vantage points (like taking a picture through a wide-angle lens). If you are having a difficult time answering any of the questions, consider what may be making it so hard.

NOTES

1. See Lazarus (1993) for a good summary of their research on the effectiveness of different coping strategies.
2. English, John, Srivastava, and Gross (2012).
3. According to our analysis, 11 of the leaders indicated that they used some version of "expect the world to be complicated and messy" as a reframe in dealing with 14 critical incidents.
4. Social psychologists refer to this phenomenon as the *fundamental attribution error*. It was first demonstrated in a classic study by E. E. Jones and Harris (1967).

5. For more on how people play the "blame game" in organizations, and the negative impact it has on individual and group performance, see Dattner and Dahl (2011).

6. Marilee Adams (2009) has done pathbreaking work on adopting an inquiring mindset. She shows how it can help people deal more effectively with many of the emotional challenges they face, both at work and in their personal lives. William Ury (1991), in his book on how to negotiate in difficult conflict situations, used the expression "going to the balcony" to describe a similar strategy for getting control of one's own emotions. He wrote that "The 'balcony' is a metaphor for a mental attitude of detachment. From the balcony you can calmly evaluate the conflict, almost as if you were a third party" (p. 17).

7. We found that 11 leaders in our study used "adopt an inquiring mindset" as a reframe in 12 different incidents.

8. Marilee Adams (2009) coined the term *judger* to refer to those whose impulse is to make judgments rather than adopt an inquiring mindset.

9. At least 11 leaders used this type of reframing in 15 situations, according to our analysis.

10. Goleman (2013, p. 76). Psychologists refer to this basic mental ability as *selective attention*.

11. Goleman (2013, p. 211).

12. For more on how moral commitment and meaning in work can help reduce stress and burnout even in highly demanding jobs, see Cherniss (1986).

13. For a critique of this perspective on what causes burnout, see Cherniss (1986).

14. Our analysis indicated that at least 10 leaders managed emotions by adopting a positive perspective in 15 situations.

15. See Seligman (2002) for a summary of the research linking optimism to many different positive outcomes.

16. Epictetus (2008).

17. Levine (2007) has published an intriguing paper on the implications of this work for psychological theory and research.

18. Pescosolido (2002).

19. Pescosolido (2002, p. 591).

20. See, for example, Schulman, Keith, and Seligman (1993).

21. For example, see Seligman's (2002) work on how it is possible to develop "learned optimism" by changing one's "explanatory style."

22. Brody (2017).

23. Cohn, Pietrucha, Saslow, Hult, and Moskowitz,(2014); Moskowitz et al. (2011).

24. Caruso and Salovey (2004, p. 112).

25. Boyatzis and McKee (2005).

26. *Confirmation bias* is the name that psychologists have given to this tendency to look for, recall, and interpret information in a way that confirms our own beliefs or hypotheses, while giving less attention and consideration to alternative explanations or possibilities. See Plous (1993).

27. The management theorist Douglas McGregor (1960) suggested more than 50 years ago that adopting a more positive perspective toward other people can be

especially useful for those in leadership positions. He observed that some leaders tend to be more pessimistic in their view of other people, seeing them as inherently lazy, lacking ambition, avoiding responsibility, and preferring to be directed by others. Other leaders have a more positive view. They believe most people want to do a good job and will work hard without much external pressure if they find the work enjoyable and meaningful. McGregor found that the managers who had a more positive view of others tended to get better results than those with a more negative view.

28. Pescosolido (2002, p. 591).
29. Seligman (2002, p. 288). Other researchers concur that the value of positive thinking depends on what one is trying to accomplish. Anxiety, for example, helps us anticipate what might go wrong. Anger can provide the energy to work for positive change. And people in a sad mood can come up with more persuasive messages than people in a happy mood. A summary of this research can be found in Caruso and Salovey (2004, pp. 101–104).
30. Seligman (2002, p. 288).
31. Dilworth and Boshyk (2010).

7

Manage Those Boundaries

magine that you are supposed to meet with a difficult customer to rene-
gotiate a contract. You have had a history of conflict with this person,
and you recognize that there is a good chance you will lose your patience at some point during the meeting. This could be highly detrimental
for your company. There are two ways in which you could manage the
emotions. First, as we described in the last chapter, you could *reframe* the
way in which you think about the situation, both before and during the
discussion, and try to maintain more emotional distance. Or, you could
modify the situation by having one of your associates, who has had an
easier time working with the customer, go to the meeting instead.

There are pros and cons to each approach, and the leaders in our study
used both; the best choice will depend on the specific situation. In the
last chapter, we looked at how the leaders managed their own emotions
and those of others by reframing the way in which they thought about
challenging situations. However, the leaders also managed emotions by

modifying the situation. In this chapter, we consider one of the strategies they often used to do so.

STRATEGY 7: CREATE OPTIMAL INTERPERSONAL BOUNDARIES

Consider the following situations:

- The director of a nursery school put into place *Robert's Rules of Order* to help manage the emotions stirred up at meetings of the parent advisory committee.
- A mid-level manager in a large cosmetics firm visited a co-worker at the co-worker's house after the co-worker's son died in an automobile accident.
- The director of a social service agency did not invite her staff to her home or go out with them. But she said she was "very interested in them," asked about them, and took "an interest when they had doctor's appointments and things like that."

Each of these examples illustrates a way in which leaders used interpersonal boundaries to help them manage their own emotions and those of others.[1] In the first example, the leader created more rigid boundaries around what people talked about and when they talked about it during meetings. In the second example, the leader loosened the boundary that normally existed between her and her team members because of the personal loss that one team member experienced. In the third example, a leader tried to establish good relations with all the staff by maintaining boundaries that were neither too rigid nor too flexible.

THE IMPORTANCE OF MAINTAINING BOUNDARIES

The importance of creating optimal interpersonal boundaries in the managing of emotion is well-understood in professions where the work can become emotionally intense and disruptive.[2] Nurses, physicians, and other medical personnel sometimes use the term *detached concern* to convey the idea that they should be caring and compassionate toward their patients while also maintaining a certain interpersonal distance. Over a period of centuries, the field of medicine has established rules and procedures designed to help medical personnel maintain an optimal balance between detachment and concern. An example is the white coat that physicians wear, which maintains a certain degree of social distance between doctor and patient while allowing considerable caring and compassion on the part of the physician. These sorts of procedures create an interpersonal boundary between the caregiver and a patient.

Organizational leaders also discover that managing interpersonal boundaries is important. Lisa Price, the founder and president of Carol's Daughter, recalled how she struggled with this aspect of the role when she first assumed a position of leadership.[3] She said that when she first became a boss, it was difficult for her to impose rules on her employees and enforce them because she "likes to be people's friend." However, when she began to impose more limits and direction on employees, she realized that many of them welcomed the tightening of boundaries.[4]

The leaders in our study managed boundaries in a number of ways. Some of the boundaries were temporary, as when the owner of a food processing company established a firm boundary between himself and a difficult customer by sending one of his associates to the meeting rather than going himself. Other boundaries were more permanent and physical, as when the director of a social service agency arranged for the program manager to move into a private office with a door that could be closed to prevent constant interruptions that were heightening her stress levels.

USING TIME OUTS TO MANAGE BOUNDARIES

Leaders often used time outs, which sometimes just involved withdrawing psychologically from the situation for a minute or so. Amy, after describing the argument she had with a group of parents, said, "When I get in situations like that, I take deep breaths. I remember calling them 'cleansing breaths' when I delivered my little girl: four in, four out." In this situation, the strategy worked; after taking a few deep breaths, Amy calmed down and ended the meeting without further escalation. After taking a week to consider the problem and various solutions, she was able to resolve it.[5]

Dorothy, the director of a small social services agency, also used time outs to help manage her emotions. When we asked her how she managed her feelings when she sometimes became frustrated and angry with staff members or volunteers, she said, "I have learned not to react immediately but to take a step back and . . . make a time to talk about it in the future, which gives me a chance to think about it." The time out is one of the simplest ways in which the leaders strengthened interpersonal boundaries in upsetting situations, and it often proved to be an effective way to manage their emotions.[6]

CREATING NEW ROLES TO MANAGE BOUNDARIES

The leaders also created new roles to establish optimal interpersonal boundaries. Amy, the nursery school director, described such a situation. It involved the development of a new website for the school. Amy knew that a particularly difficult board member would become involved in the project because that member saw herself as an expert on websites. So Amy invited the board member to take charge of the project, but she also proposed that they hire an outside consultant to do most of the work. As Amy explained, "We had to work out some system with the subcommittee so it wasn't just me and the board member having some kind of conflict. So we hired an outside consultant and set it up so the consultant was the overall supervisor." In this situation, Amy managed emotions by using roles to create a stronger interpersonal boundary between her and the tech-savvy board member. Looking back on the experience, Amy concluded, "Defining the roles that we were all playing really helped to keep this situation manageable."

USING RULES AND PROCEDURES TO CHANGE
BOUNDARIES FOR THE BETTER

In some cases, the leaders used procedures that were already in place to modify interpersonal boundaries. For instance, Doreen, another nursery school director, talked about how valuable it was to have a clear protocol to follow when one of the children in her school shows signs of abuse. She said it is always an upsetting situation, but the protocol makes it easier for both her and the teachers because there is no guesswork about whether to make the call to the child protective services agency. As she explained, "It's easier because you know that you don't have a choice. There is no choice when a child says something to you that is on the list. Then you immediately have to call protective service. You call and then they put in place what has to happen."[7]

Emotionally intelligent leaders, however, do not just rely on established institutional rules and procedures. They take the initiative and introduce new ones to help them better manage strong emotions. One example was Amy's introduction of *Robert's Rules of Order* to help create clearer boundaries during meetings of the nursery school's parents' group (see Chapter 5).

Dorothy provided another example. She established a new rule to help resolve a conflict between her program manager and the manager's new assistant. The new assistant and another staff person had been out of the office at the same time, leaving the program director alone to answer the phones. The program director, who had just returned from maternity leave, was stressed out and irritated. So Dorothy met with the program director and her assistant. After they had a chance to discuss the problem and clear the air, Dorothy "laid down some guidelines." The main one was that the two staff members would not be out of the office at the same time. If both needed to go out, they would decide who would go first.

The staff implemented the new rule. The program director no longer was left alone in the office. As a result, she became less annoyed with the other staff, and relationships in the office improved.

Dorothy also helped the program director and her new assistant come up with their own ideas for establishing better boundaries. At another point during their meeting, the program director said that the assistant should feel free to knock on her door and come in at any time. Dorothy thought that this was a bad idea because "the director was overwhelmed with work and shouldn't be interrupted too often." Also, "the assistant is a very shy person who would find it difficult to keep interrupting the director." After discussing the problem for a few minutes, the program director came up with a novel solution: Instead of knocking on her door at any time, the assistant should text her if she needed to discuss something with her. This not only turned out to be a good solution to the problem but also showed how the program director had grasped the idea of making interpersonal boundaries less loose as a way of preventing disruptive negative emotions.

The turbulent meetings of the parent committee at a nursery school, and the conflict between a program director and her assistant at a small nonprofit social service agency involved face-to-face conflicts affecting a relatively small number of people. However, there were also examples of how leaders used rules and procedures to manage the emotions of hundreds or even thousands of people. Harold, the CEO of a large supermarket chain, described in great detail how emotionally fraught his selection as the top person in the company had been (see Chapter 5). He wanted to make the process less painful for everyone when it was time to pick his successor. So with the help of an outside consultant, he came up with a more structured procedure that helped make the experience less difficult. It began with the identification of six or seven executives who seemed promising. The consultant then put the candidates through a highly structured and intensive assessment process. She also interviewed all the board members. Meanwhile, Harold met with the board on a regular basis to update it on the process, and the consultant met regularly with Harold to help him think through the issues that came up. The consultant also helped Harold develop a carefully structured process for communicating the decision once it was made.

Looking back on the experience, Harold admitted that "when it came down to a decision, it was still tough" because the outcome was unexpected and controversial. However, he believed that having a more structured process helped them manage the strong emotions not only among the candidates and Harold but also among the board members, the top management team, and virtually all of the other employees. Without such a process, "that thing would have been very confusing," in Harold's words. He believed it was especially important that "the process was laid out for the board at the outset and they agreed to it." He concluded by noting that the process they used was now used in other parts of the company.[8]

LOOSENING BOUNDARIES

Most of the examples we have considered up to this point involved tightening boundaries. However, the leaders sometimes loosened interpersonal boundaries to help members of a team better manage their emotions. Loosening boundaries also can help leaders gather valuable information. Karen, the food services manager, was able to figure out which employee blew the whistle on their company (see Chapter 6) because she had maintained a certain amount of openness in the boundaries between herself and all the employees. She said, "When I was in the units, I tried to have lunch with the unit manager and their employees. I wanted the employees to know there was an open door and if something was a problem, they certainly could come to me even if they weren't comfortable going to their boss." Having lunch with the employees on a regular basis helped Karen to better monitor the emotional climate and identify which person had been the whistle blower.

Transparency is another way of loosening interpersonal and group boundaries.[9] When Tom was the chief operating officer of a large steel company, he shared financial information about the company with all the employees at town hall meetings once each quarter. When the Great Recession hit in 2008 and the company had to close some plants, Tom believed that this transparency helped to soften the blow emotionally be-cause the workers saw it coming and understood why closing a plant was necessary. Tom said, "They may still be upset about a mill being shut down during the recession, but they know why it is being shut down and how the decision was made, and who made it. That doesn't make them happy or necessarily agree with the decision, but it makes them less upset and angry."

USING EMOTIONAL INTELLIGENCE TO ACHIEVE OPTIMAL BOUNDEDNESS

Leaders often had to tighten some boundaries while loosening others in order to maintain an optimal degree of boundedness.[10] Amy, the nursery school director, illustrated how she did this in managing her relations with members of the parents' committee. Earlier, we described how she terminated her conversation with an upset parent after a minute or two by putting off the conversation for a week. Terminating the conversation helped create a firmer boundary between her and the parent; meeting again in a week helped keep the interpersonal boundary from becoming too rigid.

Amy also loosened the boundaries between her and the parents by making sure that she regularly attended meetings of the parents' com-mittee. She said, "I need to have a different kind of relationship with the parents, one that is not adversarial. So I need to be on the parents' com-mittee." However, she pointed out that discussions in the committee also established firmer boundaries by helping the parents understand "what the boundaries are."

Achieving optimal boundedness by strengthening some boundaries while loosening others sometimes seems like walking an emotional tightrope. When Diane overlapped with another woman in her role as leader of a team, she had to use great skill in managing the psycholog-ical boundaries. The other team members did not know that their boss was being "exited" in 6 months when Diane joined the team. To ensure a positive transition, Diane had to protect the reputation and authority of the exiting team leader without weakening her own position as the new leader. And she needed to do so while maintaining a good relationship with the outgoing leader. "I had to build a trusting relationship with her so that she could trust me with information that I needed to know before she left."

Diane provided an example of how she tried to create optimal boundedness during the transition. The old leader did not want to stop leading the staff meetings, but Diane wanted to make it clear that she was ready and able to take over the leadership of the group. Diane's solution was to be more vocal in staff meetings, but to do so respectfully. At other times, Diane would just defer to the outgoing leader.

Even though Diane tried to manage the boundaries carefully, the process was not always smooth. The outgoing leader's reactions "were mixed. Some things she could let go of, and some things she couldn't." And there were times when Diane had to enlist the support of their boss. However, Diane's efforts to maintain optimal interpersonal boundaries paid off. The transition ultimately was a smooth one. The team continued to function well. Diane and the old leader were on good terms when the old leader finally left, and they continued to work together on projects and maintained a good relationship.

BOUNDARIES BETWEEN WORK AND LIFE OUTSIDE OF WORK

One of the most important boundaries for leaders to manage is the one separating work from the rest of their lives. There is a great temptation to always make work the first priority, and often the leaders have no choice but to do so. However, the leaders we studied recognized that they had to take care of themselves in order to take care of their teams and organizations. They understood that they were like parents with young children on a plane when the cabin suddenly loses air pressure and the oxygen masks drop down: Their first responsibility is to put on their own oxygen mask so that they will be strong and alert while helping their children put on their masks. In the same way, leaders need to be mentally, physically, and emotionally fit to help their groups deal with critical incidents whenever they occur. And managing the work-life boundary is crucial for doing so.[11]

Each leader found different ways to maintain a certain amount of balance in their lives, especially during challenging periods when the demands of work were unusually pressing. Diane said that she would take long walks and "embrace my family life" to help her "keep perspective on things." She also kept up her "social outlets" as a way of "letting me bitch and moan." Cynthia, the head of a large architectural and engineering firm, said, "I have found that the higher you get in an organization, the less capable you are of sharing your feelings on a bad day internally (i.e., at the office). You have to find support outside of the organization." She went on to say that she also took long walks to help restore her during the most stressful periods.

Thus, the outstanding leaders used personal and interpersonal boundaries to manage emotions in a number of ways. They often established, maintained, or tightened boundaries in order to mitigate disruptive emotions. However, they also loosened boundaries, which encouraged the expression of positive emotions, to facilitate the development of better relationships with peers, employees, bosses, or clients.

ACTIVITY 7.1: CREATING OPTIMAL BOUNDARIES

This chapter has focused on how leaders created more optimal boundaries between themselves and others, making them better able to manage distressing emotions and ultimately making them more effective in their roles. Remember Charles, the owner of a family business who had problems managing his emotions with a particularly difficult customer? To create a firmer boundary between himself and the customer, he sent one of his associates to handle the meetings rather than going himself. Yet, other leaders like Karen and Tom, worked to loosen boundaries between themselves and their co-workers by keeping the channels of communication open whether through a casual lunch or by sharing important financial information. While these leaders took their boundaries in different directions, they ultimately knew the importance of changing them to be more effective in their leadership roles.

So now it's your turn to reflect on a relationship between yourself and another person or persons that could be improved by changing the boundary that currently exists—whether that means making it firmer or more fluid. Here are some questions to get you started:

1. Think of a situation that you sometimes face in which your patience is tested by another person. You tend to become irritated, frustrated, and annoyed, and those emotions probably are making you less effective. Now consider how you might create more distance between yourself and that person so that you are able to work more easily and without as much internal or external emotional conflict. Given some of the strategies employed by the leaders in this chapter, how might you do that?

2. Think of a situation in which you would like to develop a more positive relationship with another person or group in order to facilitate communication and/or trust. It could be a peer, someone who reports to you, a client or customer, a person in another department with whom you interact, or even your boss. It also could be a group of people, such as the parents' committee at Amy's nursery school. What might you do to make the interpersonal boundary less rigid? For instance, how might you arrange to interact more with the other person or group in a positive, constructive way?

3. It's important to consider the potential ramifications of creating more optimal boundaries. What are some potential barriers or pitfalls you might encounter in implementing this approach? How might you overcome these barriers?

4. Can you enlist the help of others to aid you in creating these new boundaries?

5. How will you evaluate whether the boundaries you are creating are making things better? You might ask yourself the following questions to gauge how you are progressing: Are you feeling less stress or frustration? Are you developing a greater sense of trust in another co-worker? Are you doing less micromanaging? Do you consider your work relationships more productive and collaborative? Are you able to give and receive feedback in an honest and timely way without hesitation or dread?

NOTES

1. Eleven leaders reported using boundaries to help manage emotions in 18 incidents.
2. See, for instance, Kerasidou and Horn (2016): "The medical profession is an emotionally challenging environment, which favours the image of the emotionally detached doctor" (p. 8).
3. Bryant (2010, August 22).
4. For a more scholarly discussion of the importance of emotional distance in leadership, see Erskine (2012).
5. In their review of research on stress and coping in caregivers, Folkman and Moskowitz (2000) noted that time outs were one of the most frequently used methods for managing stress.
6. Some research suggests that it can take up to 20 minutes for people to return to baseline after they have become emotionally aroused. See Gottman (1994).
7. In a chapter on the management of destructive emotions at work, Cooper and Cartwright (2001) proposed that managers should develop policies and procedures specifically for managing emotions in organizations.
8. Perkins (2000, pp. 24–25) has described how the polar explorer Ernest Shackleton also used established routines to keep his men focused, occupied, and therefore in a positive mood most of the time when they were stranded on the ice in the Antarctic.
9. Norman, Avolio, and Luthans (2010).
10. A particularly good discussion of the importance of optimal boundedness can be found in Alderfer (1980).
11. For a thoughtful review of the topic of work-life balance in organizations, see Shobitha Poulouse (2014). See also Boyatzis and McKee (2005).

8

Enlist the Help of Others

We often credit great leaders as though they act alone. However, when it comes to managing emotions, leaders frequently receive help from others. And the best leaders understand how valuable it is to seek out others for help. George S. Barrett, chairman and CEO of Cardinal Health, had this to say about the value of others' help: "I think a leader has to be comfortable with having the weight on their shoulders. It can be hard. . . . It's not for everybody." He went on to say that he can do it—in fact, he likes it—in part because he shares the burden with others: "I like it because I don't feel I'm alone. I wind up bringing my group together, and we own the weight. I love that part of it."[1]

The outstanding leaders in our study also relied on others. They described many situations in which they reached out for help to better understand and manage emotions. It turns out that seeking out and using the help of others is often the most emotionally intelligent thing that a leader can do in critical situations.[2]

STRATEGY 8: SEEK OUT OTHERS FOR HELP
IN MANAGING EMOTIONS

In Chapter 5 we described how Amy, the director of a nursery school, instituted a modified version of *Robert's Rules of Order* after a particularly contentious meeting with the parents' committee. But Amy did not come up with this idea on her own. The administrator at the church where Amy's school was housed often conducted meetings, so Amy went to talk with her about the incident. During that conversation, the church administrator said, "Most meetings that I attend for the church follow a version of *Robert's Rules of Order*. It provides a way of addressing issues in meetings that avoids things like this from happening." She then went on to explain that under *Robert's Rules*, the contentious issue would have been brought up for the first time under "new business, at which point it would not have been discussed further that day." The church administrator also helped Amy see that it was not necessary to adopt all of *Robert's Rules* and follow it to the letter. She said, "We don't have to implement *Robert's Rules of Order* exactly. We're not some big formal organization. But the essence is that you address an issue, a brand-new issue, the following meeting. If that had been the case and we had had that rule set up, this messy confrontation never would have happened."

HOW OTHERS HELP: OFFERING ADVICE AND EMOTIONAL SUPPORT

In Amy's example, the church administrator helped her manage emotions by offering advice on how to modify the situation. However, the leaders often benefited from emotional support as well. Ruth, who was in charge of wholesale planning and operations at a large clothing manufacturer, had become embroiled in a conflict with one of her team members. The problem came to a head at their annual review meeting. Ruth recalled, "He was getting very frustrated that I couldn't sign off on some things he was requesting, and he became *very* angry. We had multiple exchanges. So the meeting didn't go very well in my book."

After the meeting ended without any resolution, Ruth found herself unable to "forgive" the employee. She also began to feel a sense of doubt about her performance as a leader. She said, "I was really taken aback. I was feeling a little defensive, and I was feeling angry that he was so angry. It really took a toll on me. It weighed heavily, and it was all I could think about day and night."

So Ruth sought out the advice of her "business coach" (an organizational psychologist who was contracted by Ruth's company to provide this kind of assistance).[3] With the coach's help, she was able to think about her feelings more fully and put together an action plan to address the problem.

> I met with my business coach about it and talked through a lot of what I was feeling and questioning. And a lot of my questions were, "What should I be doing?" "What is this all about?" "Am I OK?" "Am I allowed to feel this way?" And my coach was really great because she definitely confirmed for me that "you're only human." And she pointed out to me that his remarks and his tone of voice to me as his leader were inappropriate and disrespectful. I didn't . . . at that time, I didn't honor myself enough to realize that. So she helped me to recognize what I was truly feeling and what I needed to point out to him.

Once Ruth was able to better manage her own emotions, she could go back to the employee and deal with him more effectively. She explained, "We had a better conversation. He didn't completely apologize, but he took a step back; and he said he really did understand my point of view. He understood that there was more that he needed to consider."

When Ruth sought help from her business coach, she needed more than just a plan for how to deal with the employee. She was experiencing an emotional crisis. And in a number of ways the coach provided her with the kind of feedback, support, and encouragement that Ruth needed to manage the emotional aspects of the challenge. First, in the process of unloading some of her negative emotions, Ruth was better able to contain them. At the same time, the meeting helped Ruth to play out various options for handling the situation, which helped her feel more clear, assured, and confident in handling it. The coach's words of encouragement also provided Ruth with the optimism and hope that things would work out and be OK. And in the end, the conversation also may have helped Ruth develop greater empathy (even though she already had some) for the employee.

Reaching out to a business coach reflected considerable emotional intelligence on Ruth's part. She realized that she needed this kind of help to gain perspective on the situation. Although others in the organization thought of Ruth as someone who was especially good at managing feelings, Ruth was emotionally intelligent enough to recognize her own limitations and to go to a trusted other for both the advice and the emotional support that challenging situations often require.

Other people helped the leaders manage emotions in a number of ways. In addition to providing advice, they asked questions that helped the leaders think more clearly about the situation. They provided a sounding board that helped the leaders think through difficult situations and recognize new opportunities. And they expressed support and affirmation. In all of these ways, other people helped the leaders manage their own emotions and those of others.

SEEKING HELP FROM AN HR PARTNER DURING A ROUND OF LAYOFFS

The leaders in our study sought help from many kinds of sources. Often these sources were people within their own organization. For example, Linda, the director and vice president of product development for a large clothing company, relied on her "HR partner" for emotional support as well as technical guidance during a time when the company had to lay off a number of employees due to economic pressures. She still remembered one incident quite vividly:

So we went through that day of layoffs. We had to do a number of layoffs, and clearly that was very emotional for people. Then, after those meetings I went downstairs to meet with my team. But before I could get there, I ran into somebody on the team. She approached me in the hallway and she said, "How could you do this? How could you!" You know, screaming at me. And I said, "I understand how you feel. I understand . . ." And I just tried to calm her down. She kind of listened and calmed down a bit, and then she left.

Although Linda's team member was calmer after the incident, many of the employees continued to be upset. As Linda put it, "The next period of time was really . . . we spent a lot of time meeting with people, with individuals, with teams, talking about how they felt."

Linda was not immune to those feelings. She said that she still remembered that period "very well. . . . It was very moving, very emotional. . . . The conversations were hard, and some of the employees were really kind of nasty about the situation." Fortunately, Linda's HR partner could help her express and manage her own feelings as well as those of her team. Linda said, "We had been working closely on the layoff process, and we were able to kind of download together. . . . We were able to do a little crying together behind closed doors, which I think helped me let go."

SEEKING HELP FROM A FAMILY BUSINESS FORUM

The leaders also turned to professional help outside the organization. For Charles, the CEO of a family business, it came through a "family business forum" at a local university.[4] Charles participated regularly in programs at the forum along with several other owners of family businesses. It was a setting where they could learn from professionals, as well as from each other, how to deal with their emotions and those of their parents, siblings, and children. During our interview, Charles noted that he had "a lot of negative feelings" about his business and the family dynamics associated with it until he got involved in the family business forum. The forum helped him realize that many of the things that bothered him were patterns that repeat themselves in many family businesses. For instance, he was bothered that his father did not want to give up control of the business when he retired. He thought it was only his father who was like that, but through the forum he discovered it was "all fathers." Charles also was annoyed that his sister seemed to "grab for power wherever she could." But his annoyance dissipated when the staff at the forum helped him to see that her behavior probably arose from her feeling that she did not have any power.

Charles found it especially helpful during one session to hear from a speaker who was a psychologist and also a member of a multigeneration family business. Rather than just talk about the challenges, she spoke about all the positives associated with being part of a family business. She said that the business was "the glue that kept the family together." She went on to say that when the family finally sold their stock in the business, "there no longer was that glue, and they all lost something of value." That story helped Charles feel better about his own family business experiences.

EXECUTIVE COACHES AND PROFESSIONAL COUNSELORS AS SOURCES OF HELP IN MANAGING EMOTIONS

In a few cases, the leaders sought out executive coaches or professional counselors to help them manage their emotions. Charles said that when he was younger, he did not want to join the family business, which led to conflicts with his parents, who wanted him to do so. He felt that he was "browbeaten" by them. "My mother really laid this guilt trip on me." Charles did join the business and became president, but his resentment continued to fester, and the company suffered as a result. Charles said, "I had been with the company about two years, and we were really stagnating. I just couldn't hire new people or think of going in new directions if I were going to end up leaving." So Charles began seeing a professional counselor, and it helped him to manage his feelings. "I worked my way through it. I ended up forgiving my parents. I realized they're just human like everyone." The counseling also helped Charles to see that he really liked the company and the work, and he realized that he was very good at doing the job. He just did not like the process by which he was brought into it. Once Charles resolved his emotional conflicts with the help of the counselor, he made some key hires, and the company began to grow and flourish again.

Harold, the CEO of a large supermarket chain, did not seek out help from others either inside or outside the organization when he took over the top spot. He said, "When I became CEO, I didn't develop a network of confidants that I could talk to. I didn't have a coach. I didn't have anyone on the outside who would understand these issues. I just persevered on my own. And I think I would have avoided some early bad decisions if I had had someone to challenge me." So when it came time to pick his successor, Harold made sure he had someone with whom he could talk and who could help him think through the process. He sought the assistance of an organizational psychologist who had worked with the company on other projects, and she helped him manage all the emotions associated with selecting his successor. It turned out to be a good decision. That process, as we saw in Chapter 7, was critical in managing the emotions of board members, candidates, and other key stakeholders in the organization. Harold said, "The succession process we just went through was beautiful because I reached out and had someone own it with me." Then he added, "Strength as a CEO is asking for help."[5]

USING CAUTION WHEN SEEKING OUT HELP FROM OTHERS

In seeking additional support, the leaders in our study used their emotional intelligence in deciding whom to seek out, and how to do it safely and effectively. Michael provided a good example. He initially used an external coach to help him manage his emotions and those of others. However, his coach told him that he also needed "somebody in the company" to help him. So, with the coach's help, he identified a person who, like him, was very senior and reported to the chairman of the company. Most important, she was "completely safe . . . so she can come to me, and I can go to her." Michael then described how he initially approached this colleague to solicit her guidance and support: "So I went to this person and said, 'Look, as I'm going through all these changes with my business and growing in the company, I need somebody who can help me. But I'm not looking for a mentor, I'm looking for an equal.' And she was very open to it."

Based on this experience, Michael concluded:

> As an executive, you have to have an external coach; and you also need someone internally who understands the nuances of the company and the business and can give you a different perspective, can listen, and can say, "You know what, that's not what's going on, you're hearing it the wrong way." And I think you've got to find that because it is so incredibly valuable. There is nothing worse than being surrounded by a group of people, and you're all in competition, and you have nowhere to go. . . . *But it has to be safe; there has to be a huge amount of trust.*

Those final words are important, and they raise an equally important question: How do we know whom we can trust when we seek support and guidance from others, especially when they are part of the same organization? There does not appear to be any easy answer to this question, but it seems to be one more instance in which our emotional intelligence is vital. The leaders in our study used their ability to accurately perceive and understand emotions to determine whom they could trust to help them manage their own emotions and those of others.[6]

ACTIVITY 8.1: ASKING FOR HELP—IT'S THE EMOTIONALLY INTELLIGENT THING TO DO

This chapter was full of examples of effective leaders finding the help they needed at the time they needed it. Asking for help was a sign of emotional intelligence—not a lack thereof! Support came in different forms, both inside and outside the organization. For Charles, it was a family business forum that helped him accept and adjust to his role in the family business. For Ruth, it was an outside professional who helped her navigate a complicated work issue. And for Linda, it was an HR partner who helped her deal with the emotional and technical aspects of a company-wide layoff.

For leaders, the importance of having someone to turn to in times of need can't be overstated. Much has been studied and written about the importance of high-quality connections, which can run the gamut from bosses (current and former) to professional coaches, spouses, family members, colleagues, partners, and friends. As Murphy and Kram (prominent researchers in the field of mentoring and strategic work relationships) write, "These connections provide the social support, the sort of land bridge, to uphold your performance at work as well generate life satisfaction. Put succinctly, good relationships enable us to cope with stress and thrive during times of change."[7]

Three main questions to consider are: (a) Do you ask for help when you need it? (b) Whom do you turn to for help and support? (c) How can you continue to build quality connections that will help you survive and thrive as a leader? Let's dive into each of these questions.

1. Asking for Help

- Is asking for help easy or difficult for you?
- When are you most likely to ask for help? (For example, during a crisis, when you can't figure out what should be the next step, in working with difficult people?)
- If you find it difficult, what barrier(s) get in the way of your asking for help?
- How can you eliminate that barrier so that asking for help will come more naturally?

2. Strengthening Your Support System

Make a chart showing the people in your support system, and in what area they provide you with the most help. (For example, have a column for your Organization, Family, and Community.) Remember that the people may be both inside and outside your work organization. For example, under Organization, you might list a co-worker, a former mentor, and/or a boss. Under Community, you might include a personal friend, a teacher, an acquaintance, and/or a religious guide.

Next, consider the following questions to help you better understand the strengths of your support system and how you might make it even stronger:

- In what ways did each person's support make you a better employee and/or leader?
- Is there a current area in your life or a work situation with which you could use help?
- If so, who in your support system would be the best person for the job?
- If there is not a person on this list who could help, can you utilize your connections to enlist the help of a new person? (This provides a wonderful opportunity to expand your support system!)
- Think about how you might go about asking for their help. What is one way you can initiate contact with the person? Might you meet them for breakfast or lunch? Send them an email? Do you need an introduction first?

Remember that establishing quality connections takes time and patience. They don't happen overnight. They also don't need to be deep connections to be high-quality ones. Being proactive and taking initiative in building supportive relationships will increase your ability to develop yourself into a well-rounded and effective leader. Just take the first step and see where it leads you.

NOTES

1. Bryant (2010, August 25).
2. Thirteen leaders used this strategy in 18 of the incidents they described in the interviews.
3. There has been growing interest in the use of workplace coaching among both practitioners and scholars. For comprehensive reviews of the research on coaching, see Athanasopoulou and Dopson (2018); Bozer and Jones (2018); R. J. Jones, Woods, and Guillaume (2016); Rekalde, Landeta, and Albizu (2015).
4. For more on family forums and other types of advising to family businesses, see Strike, Michel, and Kammerlander (2018).
5. There are many models of executive coaching. Boyatzis (2007) has provided a particularly good example of how coaching can be used to help leaders develop and use their emotional intelligence. Also, see Orenstein (2007) for a different approach.
6. For a more in-depth consideration of how relationships at work can help leaders to develop emotional and social competence, see Kram and Cherniss (2001); W. Murphy and Kram (2014).
7. W. Murphy and Kram (2014, p. 19).

9

Become an Emotional Coach

Emotionally intelligent leaders are also great teachers, and many of their most important teaching efforts involve helping others to develop and use emotional intelligence. In their roles as supervisors, managers, administrators, or executives, organizational leaders are in a particularly good position to help others develop EI. People can learn about EI in training seminars and workshops, or by reading books or magazine articles, and these experiences can be helpful. People also can work with executive coaches to help them become more emotionally intelligent on the job. However, organizational leaders are more likely than trainers or coaches to see people in various real-life situations on multiple occasions over time. They also are more able to provide feedback immediately or soon after an incident. And emotionally intelligent leaders are more likely to have the kind of trusting relationship with employees that makes them more open to personal growth and development.

HELPING A WHOLE TEAM DEVELOP
EMOTIONAL INTELLIGENCE

Linda, the director and vice president of product development for a large clothing company, provided a prime example of how a leader can use her emotional intelligence to help others develop their emotional intelligence at work. She supervised a team of individuals who led their own teams. At one point, one of those individuals, Paula, was "not handling her group very well." Linda believed that helping Paula develop her ability to use her emotional intelligence abilities with her team was part of Linda's responsibility, and so it became one of her projects.

Unfortunately, Paula was not very receptive initially. When Linda first met with her to discuss the problem, Paula became "very emotional. She cried. She was like, 'How could you!' She was very, very angry." Many leaders in Linda's position might have been reluctant to embark on a developmental process with Paula at that point, and they would have backed off to minimize further conflict and stress. But Linda persisted. She believed that it was her duty to help Paula become a more emotionally intelligent leader. And she understood that the process would involve some emotionally challenging moments for Paula, but this was not necessarily a bad thing.

At first, Linda did not make much headway. Although Paula seemed to be trying, Linda could tell that she was not really getting it. "It felt to me for a long time that she was just listening to me and trying to do what I was telling her to do, but I knew that she really wasn't buying into it because I didn't see the changes in her team." Despite the lack of progress, Linda persisted for several months. Finally, Paula's performance began to improve. What ultimately led to the change is worth noting. According to Linda: "The pivotal point came when Paula became part of a team effort to reshape the company. I brought all of my team leaders into the process, and I connected with them regularly and shared . . . information with them—including confidential information—and I was more honest and transparent. I wanted them to feel part of the rebuilding effort. And throughout that whole process, Paula grew and changed." What was it about working with Paula in the context of a team learning effort? Part of it may have been that Paula was no longer the sole target, which lowered her defensiveness. It also made the learning more relevant to be applying it in the context of an actual change effort. And it is likely that other team members were open to learning, which encouraged Paula to make a more concerted effort to learn new leadership skills.

Linda's development efforts also included more direct instruction and guidance—not just for Paula but for the whole team: "I talked a lot about leadership, and gave them reading material. And we talked about some ideas that I was learning through the development programs that I was in, or from my own coach, or from books that I was reading—because I'm always reading about leadership and the psychology of interacting with people." Although it took time, Paula began to demonstrate the emotional and social competencies that Linda had been trying to help her develop. As she did so, Linda made sure to acknowledge those efforts: "And so I gave her a lot of recognition. I thanked her a lot, talked about how great she was doing. Eventually I gave her more leadership responsibility."

Helping Paula to develop her leadership abilities required a high degree of emotional and social competence on Linda's part. Paula's initial response to Linda's concern, not surprisingly, was defensive and angry. Linda, however, was not put off by this response; she was able to remain calm and positive in the face of Paula's resistance. And when Linda's efforts seemed futile, she persisted in believing that she could help Paula to change. She understood from the outset that the process would be a difficult one, so rather than lose her patience and become frustrated with Paula, she remained focused on the goal of helping her change.

STRATEGY 9: HELP OTHERS DEVELOP THEIR EMOTIONAL
INTELLIGENCE ABILITIES

Linda was not the only leader who used her emotional intelligence to help others develop and use theirs.[1] The outstanding leaders we studied believed that helping others to become more emotionally intelligent was part of their role as leaders, and they demonstrated many ways in which they used their EI to do so.

COACHING A PEER TO USE MORE EMOTIONAL INTELLIGENCE

Jonathan was one of those leaders. But in his case, the person he helped was a peer. Both Jonathan and Manny were senior executives who reported directly to the CEO in a large company that manufactured medical supplies. The company had recruited Manny about two years earlier. He was strong technically but very difficult to work with. Jonathan described him as "highly reactive emotionally . . . loud . . . highly opinionated . . . rough around the edges." Because the CEO viewed Jonathan as a particularly skillful and sensitive leader, he asked him to help Manny become more emotionally competent.

Jonathan began by observing Manny's behavior in different situations. He realized that Manny "would think something and it would just come out of his mouth. He was not able to stop himself, and he was not aware of what he was doing." Manny also did not seem to be able to read his environment. He would tell off-color jokes "in an environment where it was clearly unacceptable." Jonathan then added, "Our environment is not the kind where we do things fast and loose. It's not a locker-room kind of environment."

After Jonathan had spent some time studying the causes and effects of Manny's problematic behaviors, he began to work with him. Jonathan explained, "My early endeavors were to raise Manny's awareness, to reflect on the inappropriateness of his behavior, and to call attention to the circumstances in which it occurred—just to dissect it." Jonathan was careful to meet with Manny one-on-one and to do so "as quickly and as proximately to the behavior as I could. I would say to Manny, 'Look, here is what I observed, and here is what I am hearing from others in the organization. Are you aware that you are doing this? Or how you are being perceived?' "

Unfortunately, Manny's initial reaction was not helpful. He did not deny his behavior, but he minimized it. Meanwhile, Jonathan continued to try to better understand why Manny acted as he did. He realized that Manny "had behaved this way in other organizational cultures and had never been called on it."

Like Linda, Jonathan had to be patient and persistent because Manny did not respond positively to his efforts for some time. According to Jonathan, "Initially, he would listen and then disregard it. He seemed to think that I would just go away and accept his behavior. But I didn't. I kept coming back to him." Although Jonathan was patient, Manny was not. After two or three of these discussions with Jonathan, Manny told Jonathan "quite blank that I was out of bounds and that I had no right to question his approach or behavior. And he gave me the finger and told me to leave his office!" However, Jonathan managed to avoid taking it personally. He realized that Manny "was used to being abusive and to attack." Rather than engaging in a counterattack, Jonathan made a concerted effort "not to respond."

Jonathan's patience and persistence eventually paid off. The turning point came when he discovered a way to develop a more positive relationship with Manny:

> In parallel to some of these incidents going on, Manny was having some problems in respect to his relocation from another state: He was concerned about how much money he would lose selling his old home and buying a comparable one here. At one point, he actually came to one of my colleagues and said, "I don't know if this is going to work. I think I'm going to have to leave. I'm better off going back to my former employer to see if they would take me back than to stay here. I obviously don't fit in and it will cost me an arm and leg to make this work."

Jonathan looked for ways to ease the financial burdens associated with Manny's relocation, and eventually he was able to get the company to do some things that were "costly and beyond what we had committed to do to help Manny with his relocation expenses." These actions "addressed Manny's immediate anxiety, and that just presented a huge relief for him."

Manny gave Jonathan all the credit for the company's additional help with the relocation problems, and "it went a long, long way toward his changing his perspective and not seeing me as the enemy." Now when Jonathan gave him feedback, Manny really listened. He would even "stop in my office and ask for advice or feedback." Eventually, Manny asked Jonathan if he could "line up some executive coaching" for him. Jonathan gladly complied.

The coaching included a "360-degree assessment," which gave Manny "some fairly good data from a variety of different views, so it wasn't just from me."[2] Manny digested the feedback with the help of his coach and developed an action plan. The plan dealt not only with some areas of technical effectiveness but also with better emotional control and professionalism. As Jonathan recalled, "It created an atmosphere where we could build upon the initial trust, which continued to deepen."

Helping Manny develop greater emotional intelligence in the way he handled his interactions with others took a long time, and the process was not smooth or easy. But ultimately it was successful. Jonathan concluded his story by noting that Manny had recently done "an absolutely terrific presentation to the board of directors. And the next day, as soon as I saw him walk by, I went into his office to tell him how proud I was of him, how he had distinguished himself and how he had served not just himself but the entire team. The guy just beamed with pride!"

SPECIFIC EI ABILITIES NEEDED IN COACHING OTHERS TO USE THEIR EI

Jonathan used several key EI abilities in his work with Manny. He began by carefully observing Manny's behavior in different contexts, which led to a more precise identification of how Manny's emotions got in the way of his performance and affected others. As he continued to observe and monitor

Manny's emotional volatility, Jonathan's understanding deepened. He recognized the important role that the social context played. He realized that Manny's behavior probably was less of a problem in his previous work settings because the organizational cultures were different. Jonathan also came to understand that the financial stresses caused by Manny's relocation contributed to his emotional problems. Jonathan's acute awareness and understanding of the emotional dynamics in Manny's case helped him to pinpoint the areas where Manny needed help.

During the development process, Jonathan needed to use his EI to manage his own emotions as well as Manny's. When Manny verbally attacked him at one point, Jonathan resisted the impulse to retaliate. He used several of the reframing techniques we discussed in Chapter 6, such as keeping in mind how the situation contributed to Manny's abusive behavior rather than putting all the blame on Manny, adopting an inquiring mindset toward Manny's behavior, and keeping his focus on the primary task of helping Manny to change. As time passed and there was little improvement in Manny's behavior, Jonathan was able to persist because he recognized from the outset that the change process would be complicated, messy, and protracted. Jonathan also demonstrated great skill in using techniques such as feedback to help Manny change. He understood that the feedback would have to be provided repeatedly and that it needed to be as specific as possible. It also had to be delivered very soon after the behavior occurred. And Jonathan also understood how important it was to provide not just negative feedback but also positive feedback whenever he saw Manny manage his emotions effectively.[3] But, perhaps most important, Jonathan recognized how vital it was to create "an atmosphere of trust," and he used his EI to do so.

Jonathan's work with Manny was challenging in part because he and Manny were peers. Other leaders in our study also described situations in which they helped peers, and some even helped their bosses to develop greater emotional intelligence. Helping one's boss to lead with more emotional intelligence requires even greater skill and sensitivity. However, if leaders spent more time trying to help their bosses and peers to develop greater emotional intelligence, rather than just complaining about their lack of it, it could improve both the organizational climate and perfor-mance. It requires considerable emotional intelligence, but for leaders who possess those abilities, it can be one of the most important ways in which they use them.

USING A MORE FORMAL MECHANISM TO HELP LEADERS IN A COMPANY USE MORE EI

The outstanding leaders usually helped others develop their EI informally on the job, as was the case with Linda's and Jonathan's examples. However, in a few instances they used more formal structures for doing so. Cynthia, the CEO of a large engineering firm, described how she helped others develop greater EI through a group-based program established by her company. The groups met once monthly for 90 minutes and were led by organizational leaders, including Cynthia. The groups grew out of an emotional intelligence development program that the company had launched some time earlier.

The group served multiple purposes. According to Cynthia, "It was a way to reinforce what you learned in the class on emotional intelligence. And it also created a safe place for people to talk about how they are feeling. . . . It's like a level of emotional support but guided always with an eye toward how we can improve, and what does it mean for the business when we do that?"

The company leaders who co-led the discussion groups received special training, a resource guide, and ongoing support and guidance from professional consultants to help them create a safe atmosphere in the group. As Cynthia noted, "A lot of the group depends on the leader, and we coach the leaders."

To help the employees in her discussion group use what they learned back on the job, Cynthia and the other group leaders repeatedly pointed out to them how they could do so. For instance, after helping her group members during one session explore their feelings about recent changes in the company, Cynthia said to them, "What we just did is an example of how you can help our employees in a positive way make the changes we need to do without having it be negative."

The discussion groups provided another way for leaders like Cynthia to use their EI to help others develop their own EI. And it was a particularly powerful way of doing so because it was a formal, ongoing, organization-wide process that involved the top leadership in a direct, hands-on way. How successful such an innovation would be in other settings remains to be seen, but in Cynthia's mind, the groups were a success in her company: "The average employee appreciates the opportunity to sit with a leader of the company and talk about things. So I think it has worked well in our environment."

CONCLUSION

Helping others to develop emotional intelligence competencies is another way in which the leaders in our study used their EI, and they saw this as a vital part of the leadership role.[4] The development efforts were often embedded in their day-to-day work, which made those efforts especially effective. Naturally occurring situations can be particularly fertile for helping people to develop emotional intelligence because they generate greater motivation and receptivity. They also are good for learning because the leaders have multiple opportunities to see the other person in real-life situations and to give feedback and support.[5]

However, having many opportunities to help others develop EI abilities was not sufficient. The leaders' own EI helped them to use these naturally occurring situations *effectively*. Their EI enabled them to have greater credibility and authority, which made others more receptive to the leaders' development efforts. In Jonathan's work with Manny, for example, he had to control his own emotions in response to Manny's abusive behavior toward him early in the process. Then his emotional insight helped him to better understand the underlying causes of Manny's problematic behavior. Based on that understanding, he was able to help Manny resolve a major source of anxiety in his life, which dramatically changed Manny's receptiveness.

The leaders' ability to persist in the face of setbacks and resistance also was especially critical when they helped others to develop greater EI. Even though the leaders in our study were highly respected and admired by people who worked with them, their efforts to help others develop EI often did not seem to have any impact initially. And in several instances, progress was scant for a long time. But the leaders persisted, and eventually the other person began to change.[6]

Another theme that emerged from these incidents involved the importance of the team and organizational culture in supporting the development of EI by the leaders. Cynthia's engineering company had a major, multi-year commitment to making emotional intelligence a core part of its culture. The company hired an outside consulting firm that developed an in-house training program and provided extensive coaching for leaders at all levels. The innovative use of discussion groups helped make the intervention even more far-reaching. And strong, visible support from the CEO and other members of the top leadership team reinforced those efforts. (For more on the role of organizational culture, see Chapter 11.)

For other leaders, the efforts to create a supportive culture for EI development were more modest but important nonetheless. Linda, after working with one member of her team on developing EI, brought it to another level as she began to work on it with the entire team as part of a major organizational change effort. Dorothy helped her staff develop greater EI in the way she worked with them to resolve conflicts and deal with other personal and interpersonal challenges in their day-to-day work.

Thus, what made the leaders we interviewed outstanding was not just the way they used their emotional intelligence but also their commitment to helping others develop EI. The leaders saw it as an important part of their jobs, and they found many opportunities to do so. Even when their efforts met with some initial resistance, which was often the case, they persisted. And they continually looked for ways to create not just more emotionally intelligent people but also more emotionally intelligent teams and organizations. In this way they brought out the best in others, which is ultimately the best way to use one's emotional intelligence.

ACTIVITY 9.1: LEARNING FROM A TEACHABLE MOMENT

Did you ever have a moment when someone had a big impact on your emotional development, and it changed the way you thought or responded from that point on?

One of the authors of this book had such a teachable moment. It was a short moment, maybe even unremarkable to an outsider, but it made a tremendous impact at a time when she needed it most. Maybe it has even happened to you—being late to an appointment when it is out of your control. It began with her husband being delayed at work and not being able to get home in time to take over the care of their 3-year-old son. Tired from a day of watching a toddler and feeling stressed from the negative thoughts and emotions filling her head as she drove to her meditation class (e.g., I'm angry with my husband for making me late, this was a dumb idea, the teacher will be annoyed with me, they'll think I'm a slacker), the author became filled with dread as she slowly opened the door to the meditation room. She expected to be reprimanded for disrupting the class. But something else happened that both surprised and changed her. The meditation teacher, sitting on the floor, looked straight up at her and with a smile told her to come in and relax in the space that they had made for her. The teacher even made a comment that it looked like meditation was exactly what the doctor ordered! Relieved, the author took her place and apologized for being late. Within moments, the harsh judgments and conversations that were going on in her head dissipated, allowing her to focus on the teacher's instructions. Later the teacher shared her experience of practicing meditation as she raised her own young children. The author was eternally grateful for the teacher's empathy and caring. She also learned not to be such a harsh critic of herself and others, and she still tries to practice meditation—something that doesn't always come easily!

So now it's time for you to think about a time when an individual had a positive impact on your emotional development.

- How did it occur?
- What stood out about the moment?
- What impact did it have on you?
- What made it a teachable moment?

And just as this chapter was about helping others learn and develop their emotional intelligence, how might you take what you've learned from your example and use it to create a "teachable moment" for someone else?

ACTIVITY 9.2: BUILDING TRUST

Trust is essential for helping people to change in emotionally intelligent ways. Leaders like Linda and Jonathan built an atmosphere of trust by doing such things as resisting the urge to retaliate, being more transparent, giving sincere and caring feedback, and including others in important conversations, which in turn allowed their people to develop into stronger and competent leaders themselves.

There is no doubt that building trust takes time and can be difficult. Paradoxically, we sometimes have to trust what hasn't been proved trustworthy yet. But effective leaders are willing to engage in the trust-building process because they know it is the only way to truly harness the talents, skills, and loyalty of the people who work with them and to get the kind of results that allow an organization to thrive.

The following exercise is a chance to reflect on how trust operates in your own relationships and to discover what factors come into play in helping you build more effective and connected relationships.

Take a few moments to think about a relationship (work or personal) in which there is trust, and allow yourself to reflect on the following:

1. Try to identify what the other person did to help build that trust with you. (I.e., Did they follow through on what you asked of them? Were they able to communicate their emotions in a way that felt nonthreatening? Did they share a common experience/history with you? Did they admit their mistakes?)
2. What did you do to build that relationship of trust?
3. What factors, in your opinion, destroy trust or make it difficult to trust? (To help you answer this question, you might want to recall a relationship in which there was very little trust.)
4. Have you ever had a relationship in which you had to rebuild trust? What allowed that to happen?

Trust builds positive relationships, and positive relationships build better futures. Given that there are many things that are beyond our control, what might be in your control in developing greater trust with a particular person (or group) in the future?

NOTES

1. Thirteen leaders in our study described 15 incidents in which they used this strategy.
2. A "360-degree assessment" asks people in different roles to describe the leader's behavior. It usually includes the person's bosses, peers, and direct reports. Sometimes clients, customers, friends, or family members are included as well. It is called a "360" because it provides a more rounded view of the person than just a rating by a boss.
3. Jonathan also used many other specific techniques that are presented in Cherniss and Adler's (2000) book on how to help people develop emotional intelligence.
4. Research supports this view: "Developing others" emerged as one of the 12 most important emotional and social competencies for leaders in dozens of competency

studies performed over many years. The studies were done by the Korn Ferry/Hay Group consulting firm. See Boyatzis (2009); Goleman, Boyatzis, and McKee (2002).

5. See McCall (2013); McCall, Lombardo, and Morrison (1988).
6. Research has repeatedly confirmed that persistence is a significant success factor. For two perspectives on this work, see Credé, Tynan, and Harms (2017); Duckworth and Seligman (2005).

10

Emotional Virtuosity

Using Several Strategies Together

In each of the previous chapters we described how the outstanding leaders in our study used *one* of the emotional intelligence strategies. However, the leaders typically used several strategies together in dealing with a critical challenge or opportunity. And the way in which the leaders combined strategies was as important for their success as was their skill in using any particular strategy by itself. In this chapter we highlight how the leaders did so in several specific incidents.

TOM: "WHAT THE HELL AM I GOING TO DO?"

We began this book with the story of Tom, who, as a young engineer and new team leader in a large steel company, had to face a barrage of criticism at a meeting with a major customer just a week after assuming his new position. He was totally unprepared to learn that his team was "lousy at everything." He thought, "Oh, my God, what the hell am I going to do?" Along with his fear, he also became angry at his team: "I thought about how my guys had been in the business for a while, and I thought, 'What the hell have you been doing?'" So Tom first had to manage his own emotions.

Tom began by using *Strategy 3 (Consider how your own behavior influences others' emotions)*. He remembered something he had learned early in life and thought of often: "You just can't react viscerally every time something comes up because it just scares people away." This EI strategy helped Tom begin to manage his emotions at the meeting, but it was only the first step in a process.

Tom also used *Strategy 6 (Reframe how you think about the situation)* by reminding himself that *the world is complicated and messy*. This situation was just confirmation of that basic truth. He also remembered that a primary part of his role as both an engineer and a manager was to deal with messy situations and figure out how to fix them. As Tom modified the way he thought about the situation and his role, he began to feel calmer and was able to *focus on the task at hand*, another strategy that helped him to feel even less upset.

As Tom's initial emotional agitation subsided, he was able to move to the next part of the process, which was to manage the emotions of the other company's representatives. This required that he attend not only to what they were saying but also to their feelings. He did this by using *Strategy 4 (Put yourself in others' shoes)*. He actually said to the reps, "If I were you, I wouldn't blame you if you fired us as a supplier." This disarming, empathic statement also employed *Strategy 7 (Manage emotions by working with interpersonal boundaries)*. It helped break down the rigid interpersonal boundary between the other company's people and Tom and his team. It showed them that Tom had heard them, and he understood how upset they were about the situation. Tom then ended on a positive note, saying, "But if you give us a chance to fix these problems, I guarantee you that we will not have this kind of meeting next year" (another use of *Strategy 6: Reframe how you think about the situation*). Emotions are contagious, and Tom's conviction that the situation would improve, delivered in just the right way after acknowledging the seriousness of the problem, helped convince the company representatives to give Tom and his team another chance.

When Tom met with his team the next day to debrief and decide what to do next, he again used some of the EI strategies. Most important, *he did not play the blame game*; instead, he *adopted an inquiring mindset* and *focused on the task at hand* (three reframes—*Strategy 6*). Even when some of the team members complained about how the company and their previous boss let them down, Tom resisted the impulse to cut them off and shift the blame back on them. As he put it, "My focus was not on beating anyone up." Instead, he just listened. He again used the strategy of *putting himself in others' shoes* and recognized that the team was as upset as he was and needed an opportunity to vent their feelings. When he sensed that they had vented enough, he used one more reframe: He *switched the focus to the goals and the task at hand* by saying, "OK. So what can we do to fix this?"

The way in which Tom used his emotional intelligence followed a certain pattern, which is displayed in Figure 10.1. Of course, in real-time situations, the process is more complex. Rather than a simple linear progression from awareness, understanding, and management of his feelings to awareness, understanding, and management of others' feelings, it likely was more of a back-and-forth process. Tom may have thought first about his own feelings but then switched to thinking about how others were feeling; then he thought about how he might take control of the emotional dynamics, then switched back to consider why he was feeling the way he was, and so on. However, we think that the general pattern was to do more perceiving and thinking about feelings initially and then focus

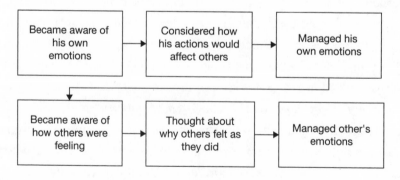

Figure 10.1 How Tom combined the emotional intelligence abilities

more on how to act in ways that would move those feelings in a direction that helped Tom deal effectively with the situation. Also, while Tom went back and forth between his own feelings and those of others, the general flow was for him to focus more on understanding and managing his own emotions and then, as he began to feel calmer, focus more on understanding and managing the emotions of others.[1]

CYNTHIA: "THIS IS REALLY GOOD! TELL ME HOW YOU DID THIS"

Cynthia, the CEO of an engineering firm with more than 150 employees, provided another example of how a leader skillfully combined several of the EI strategies. She talked at length about how the firm dealt with the aftershock of laying off about 10% of its employees during the height of the 2008 recession (see Chapter 1). Even before the announcement was made, she talked with all the directors "to see where they were emotionally with this" (*Strategy 1: Monitor the emotional climate*). Some of them were "right on board." However, Cynthia could see that "a couple of them were really struggling with it." So she met with them and approached the discussions with an inquiring mindset (*Strategy 8: Seek out others for help in managing emotions*). When one of the directors said, "Oh, let's hold on a little bit more, I'm really feeling like I can't let this person go," Cynthia didn't try to argue with her. She encouraged her to adopt an inquiring mindset by calmly asking, "Well, can you tell me a little bit more about this?" After the director had a chance to express her feelings concerning the layoffs and seemed ready to think about the options and consequences, Cynthia gently pointed out that the person they were discussing did not have any work to do. Looking back on the discussions, Cynthia acknowledged that it took more time to use these EI strategies with the reluctant directors, but "it would have taken more time to try to jam something down, and the cleanup would have been bad."

Cynthia continued to monitor the emotional climate in one-on-one interactions and group meetings after the layoffs were announced. The weekly meetings of the top leadership group were particularly bleak as one bit of bad news followed another. As Cynthia monitored the emotional climate and its impact on the group, she noticed that the team members were leaving the room at the end of each meeting "with long faces." She understood that emotions—especially those of a group's leaders—are contagious. So at the next meeting she mentioned to the team what she had observed and urged them to try to look less sad and worried in the future when their meetings end and they leave the room (*Strategy 3: Consider how your own behavior influences others' emotions*).

However, it is difficult to express positive emotions effectively if one does not genuinely feel them, so Cynthia looked for ways to lift the mood of the leadership group during their meetings. After many weeks of negative financial reports, the group learned during one of their meetings that the company had exceeded the weekly target for revenue. However, Cynthia noticed that the team members took the news "matter-of-factly" and quickly moved on to the next item on the agenda. So she stopped them and said, "You know, this is really good! Tell me how you did this" (*Strategy 6: Reframe how you think about the situation*). It worked. As the team members told Cynthia and the others how they did it, she could see them "become more animated about the success."

Cynthia also used *Strategy 2* (*Express your feelings to motivate others*) at several points during the layoff process and its aftermath. For instance, following the announcement of the layoffs, she began her crucial meeting with all of the remaining employees by expressing her own sadness over what had to be done, and letting them know that she was available to meet with them individually if they wished.

Like Tom, Cynthia used several different EI strategies to help her organization deal with the emotions associated with a major challenge. In her case, monitoring the emotional climate was the foundation and starting point. Becoming aware of how individual employees were reacting then led to the use of one or more other EI strategies to help her and others better understand and manage their feelings. This process is shown in Figure 10.2.

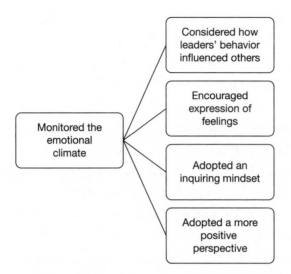

Figure 10.2 How Cynthia combined the emotional intelligence strategies

HAROLD: "WHAT AM I GETTING MYSELF INTO HERE?"

Harold, the CEO of a large supermarket chain, also used several of the EI strategies when he managed two leadership transitions during his career (see Chapters 2 and 5). The first was when he became the CEO of his company. At that point, he was the first non–family member in the long history of the company to take the top position,; and his predecessor, who had been the CEO for many years, was "something of a legend." The pressures on Harold were enormous. He still remembered sitting at the retirement celebration for his predecessor, a highly emotional event attended by more than 2,000 employees, and thinking, "What am I getting myself into here?"

Harold began by managing his own emotions. He initially relied on *Strategy 6 (Reframe how you think about the situation)*, reminding himself of the positive aspects of the situation and what he had going for him. He found it particularly helpful to remind himself that the board had endorsed him, and he had the support of a majority of the employees. As he felt less stressed out about the situation, Harold was able to put himself in others' shoes and think about how others in the organization felt about the situation (*Strategy 4*). He realized that many employees had "a very strong emotional attachment" to the company and "did not accept change very easily," and that they would be concerned about how much he would challenge the company's culture. He said, "I knew that I wouldn't be accepted unless I showed great reverence for the traditions and values that had made this company what it is" (*Strategy 3: Consider how your own behavior influences others' emotions*). This empathic awareness and understanding helped him to *decipher the underlying emotional dynamics of the situation* (*Strategy 5*); based on this, Harold developed an approach that was consistent with his style and vision for the company but also compatible with the company's culture.

Harold's company thrived under his leadership, and 8 years later, when he was ready to retire, he enjoyed widespread support from the board and the employees. Nevertheless, he remembered that he did make mistakes during the transition. Because he was someone who set high standards for himself, these mistakes could have shaken Harold's self-confidence and disrupted his emotional equilibrium. However, Harold was "a big believer" in learning from his mistakes. Thus, rather than deny that he made mistakes or just shrug them off and move on, Harold adopted an inquiring mindset (*Strategy 6: Reframe how you think about the situation*) in order to learn from them. And he applied what he learned when it was time to pick his own successor.

One of the most important lessons was that he needed the help of others (*Strategy 8: Seek out others for help in managing emotions*). He regretted that when he had become the CEO, he did not "develop a network of confidants that I could talk to." There was no one to help him understand the issues or challenge him. So he resolved that when it was time to pick his successor, he would have someone there with whom he could confer on a regular basis. He used an organizational psychologist who had worked with the company on other issues in the past. She helped him think through issues and plan at every stage of the process. With her help, the process went much better than it had when he took over as CEO. In particular, the delicate emotional dynamics involving the internal candidates who did not get the job were handled better.

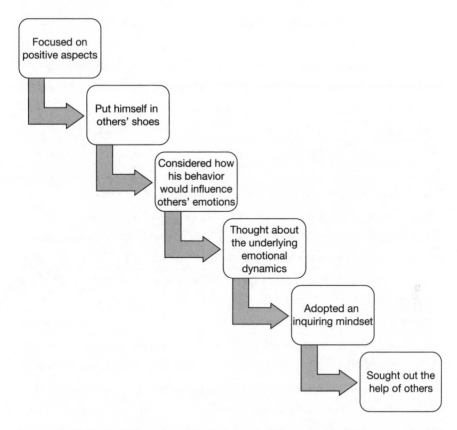

Figure 10.3 How Harold combined the emotional intelligence strategies

Harold thus used a number of EI strategies to help him deal with the emotional challenges of leadership succession. One way to depict how he orchestrated these strategies is presented in Figure 10.3.

KAREN: "SHE WAS JUST TERRIBLY, TERRIBLY ANGRY"

Many of the leaders used reframing (*Strategy 6*) to manage their emotions and those of others, but they usually combined it with several other strategies. Karen, the corporate food services manager, used almost every EI strategy when she had to deal with an employee who had falsely accused their company of violating federal health and safety regulations (see Chapters 3, 6, and 7). She began by narrowing down which employee was the accuser. Fortunately, Karen had been *monitoring closely the emotional climate* in her group (*Strategy 1*) and noted that there had been a change in the behavior of one employee: a woman who normally was outgoing and friendly but who recently had become reluctant to talk, "erratic" in her behavior, and "agitated over minor things."

Once Karen believed she knew who had made the false report, she became angry; in fact, she said she wanted to "strangle her!" She recognized, however, that expressing her anger so strongly could be counterproductive. "I stepped back and realized it was totally inappropriate for me to act angry or upset or frustrated because I wasn't going to be able to identify the problem (*Strategy 3: Consider how your own behavior influences others' emotions*). And I guess part of me thought this could be related to a personal problem the employee had, and with an open dialogue I could help with this problem."

So the next task for Karen was to manage her anger. She used two reframing techniques to do so (*Strategy 6*). First, she *backed away from playing the blame game* and reminded herself that situational influences could be contributing to the woman's behavior. To determine what they might be and further de-escalate her anger, Karen also *adopted an inquiring mindset*. She arranged to meet with the employee—not to accuse or reprimand her, but to learn more about what was going on in the employee's life. She saw it as a fact-finding meeting, and she maintained a friendly, sympathetic, and interested demeanor throughout.

The employee initially responded brusquely, with one-word answers and no explanations. However, when Karen asked her if she was getting ready for the holidays, the woman suddenly erupted: "She literally started screaming at me that she couldn't take the holidays this year and didn't I understand that?" Karen maintained her calm, sympathetic tone and said, "No, I don't understand, but holidays are tough for many people" (*Strategy 2: Express your feelings to influence others and develop more positive relationships*). At that point, the employee "completely broke down crying and indicated that her husband had just been diagnosed with cancer and she couldn't understand why this was happening to them."

One of Karen's goals during the conversation was to break down the rigid interpersonal boundary that had developed between her and the employee, and her persistence, patience, and sympathy had helped her to do so (*Strategy 7: Manage emotions by working with interpersonal boundaries*). The employee now was willing to share more information with Karen. She said that she and her husband were estranged from their closest relatives and did not have any close friends. Also, they had not been able to get any clear information from the doctors.

Karen now could put herself in the employee's shoes and see what the situation was like for her (*Strategy 4*): "What I got from her was that she and her husband had no understanding of what was involved and saw this as a death sentence. And she was just terribly, terribly angry." Once she understood the employee's situation, Karen was able to figure out why the employee had made the false accusation: "My anger at her at that moment dissipated because I understood where it came from. She was just angry with life and had no outlet for that anger. So I ascertained that she made the complaint [against our company] as an outlet for this anger" (*Strategy 5: Decipher the underlying emotional dynamics of the situation*).

After Karen discovered what the problem was, she became more sympathetic toward the employee and was able to help her deal with both the emotional and the practical issues associated with the illness; with Karen's help, the employee was able to get more support from others in her life. "She also was able to get some information to guide her husband through the process the doctors outlined for him, and she was able to get to the point where she and her husband could ask questions." Also, focusing on the practical tasks at hand helped Karen manage her own emotions, and it helped the employee better manage hers as well.

In addition, Karen used *Strategy 9* (*Help others develop their emotional intelligence abilities*): "I also brought up how her behavior had been a little erratic and how she was getting upset over small things, not understanding directions, etc. And she said, 'It's definitely related to this. I'm just wound so tight that any little thing is throwing me for a loop.'"

Karen also had to get her bosses to use more emotional intelligence in the way they handled the situation. She said they initially wanted to fire the woman. However, Karen helped them to respond in a more emotionally intelligent way (*Strategy 9*). She said to them, "No, we're not going to do that. We're going to put her in a better place and hopefully she'll return to the productive employee that she was before." One reason Karen was able to manage her bosses' emotional reactions was that she had sought out the help of the company's human resources group beforehand. She said, "I knew upper management was going to be hostile, so I went to corporate human resources first and told them the situation. That way, when I said to my bosses, 'We can't do that,' I knew they were going to hear the same thing from HR" (*Strategy 5: Decipher the underlying emotional dynamics of the situation*).

However, there was still the matter of the violations and fines that the employee's complaint had brought down on the company. Initially, many people tried to dissuade Karen from appealing the fines: "So many others within the food service industry were saying, 'Once you get a violation from OSHA [the Occupational Safety and Health Administration], that's it, they won't listen to you." Even Karen's bosses were reluctant to fight it. But Karen felt strongly that they had been unjustly accused, and so she convinced her bosses to let her put together an appeal and go to court. And they won.

Looking back on that victory, Karen said, "I think it was my passion and determination, and the fact that the charges weren't legitimate, that helped us to win it." She also noted that she was especially effective in presenting their case because "I tried to put myself in the shoes of the inspectors [*Strategy 4*]; and I was very factual, very professional, accurate, and complete when I was in court with them. And when we walked out afterward there were no ill feelings; in fact, they indicated that I was correct and they appreciated my thoroughness."

Karen's achievement illustrated again that top leaders use more than one EI strategy to deal with a challenge. This complex use of a variety of EI strategies is summarized in Figures 10.4a and 10.4b.

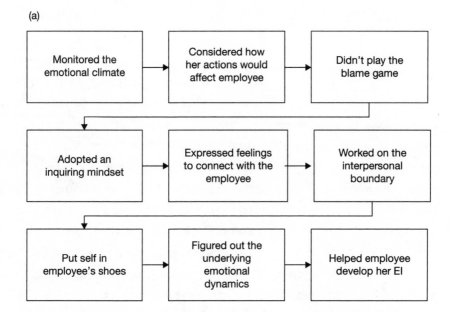

Figure 10.4a How Karen combined the emotional intelligence strategies in working with the employee

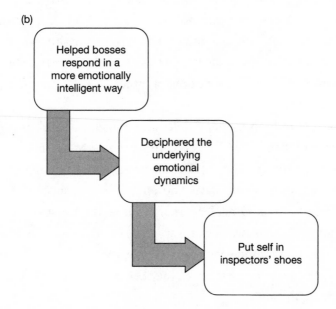

Figure 10.4b How Karen combined the emotional intelligence strategies in working with her bosses and the federal agency

CONCLUSION: SO MANY WAYS TO PUT
IT TOGETHER

In this chapter we have seen that effective leadership depends on how well leaders combine and use the EI strategies when dealing with different kinds of situations. While the leaders combined various strategies in different ways, they tended to use some strategies more than others. Most often, the leaders used *Strategy 3 (Consider how your own behavior influences others' emotions)*; 22 of the 25 leaders in our study used the strategy in 35 different incidents. In this chapter, we saw how Tom used the strategy to remind himself that "reacting viscerally" when he was the target of criticism from his company's major customer would have a negative impact. Cynthia used the same strategy to help her realize that her leadership team needed to leave their weekly meetings feeling less depressed. For Harold, the strategy helped him to make his transition as CEO by reminding him that his attitudes toward the company's traditions and values would be reflected in his behavior, which would strongly affect the employees' response to him. And Karen, like Tom, realized that she had to modulate her anger toward the employee who had filed a false claim against their company when she met with the employee to resolve the situation in a positive way. Whatever other strategies these leaders used, understanding how their behavior affected the emotions of others was key in each of these critical incidents.[2]

Leaders not only used many different strategies in each incident but also combined them in varied ways. Tom seemed to begin by becoming more aware of his emotions, followed by an understanding of the impact those emotions could have, and ending with a successful effort to manage the emotions. Other leaders also followed this pattern in many of the incidents.[3] But this was not always the case. For instance, the leaders sometimes seemed to manage their emotions *first* rather than last. Then, once they felt calmer and less upset, they could begin to better understand the emotional dynamics.

The process of using the EI strategies also was not a linear one. The leaders might use a particular EI strategy multiple times at different points in an incident. Karen and Tom, for example, demonstrated how the leaders often returned to managing emotion several times during the course of an incident. And monitoring the emotional climate was a strategy that the leaders often used continually.

Finally, it would be overly simplistic to assume that the leaders were consciously thinking about how they were using the different strategies during an incident. Sometimes the leaders were able to recognize the strategies as they described the incidents during our interviews, as when Karen mentioned that she tried to put herself in the inspectors' shoes when she was preparing for the appeal hearing. However, this was in hindsight. It was only later that the leaders looked back and became aware of some of the steps in the process and how they fit together.

NOTES

1. Pescosolido (2002), in his study of how emergent leaders managed the emotions of their groups, discovered that they followed a similar pattern. He wrote, "I propose that group leaders manage group emotional responses by first empathizing and identifying with the collective emotional state of group members, and understanding what factors in the situation are causing this emotional state. They then craft a response to the situation that is causing the emotional reaction, and communicate their response to the group both verbally and by taking action" (p. 586).
2. The leaders in our study used *Strategy 5 (Decipher the underlying emotional dynamics of the situation)* next most often: 18 leaders used it in 28 incidents.
3. In EI research, some of the most influential thinkers have suggested that people generally follow this linear process. See, for example, Goleman (2001); Joseph and Newman (2010); Mayer and Salovey (1997).

11

Creating a Social Context That Supports Emotional Intelligence

A leader's emotional intelligence will affect how well he or she uses the EI strategies to deal effectively with critical challenges and opportunities. However, the social and organizational context often affects whether leaders can even use the strategies. Some settings encourage leaders to use their EI while others do the opposite. Fortunately, there are many ways in which organizations can support the use of EI, and many examples of how they have done so.

THE IMPACT OF ORGANIZATIONAL CULTURE ON A LEADER'S USE OF EMOTIONAL INTELLIGENCE

The culture of a setting is a critical part of the social context influencing whether leaders will use their EI. Within any group or organization, social norms develop that either reward or punish emotionally intelligent behavior. A study that examined the construction industry in the United Kingdom found it to be a "male-dominated culture" that values "aggressive management styles."[1] Semistructured interviews with project managers revealed an occupational culture that discourages them from using emotional intelligence even though many of them endorsed the need for it.

Other kinds of organizations also view brashness and hard-hitting behaviors as signs of strength. They value short-term results more than long-term, and they emphasize ends over means. As Boyatzis and McKee note, "Being smart, quick, and efficient in meeting objectives is prized."[2] Achievement is overvalued, and people become "mindlessly focused on getting things done."[3] Alex Soojung-Kim Pang observed, "With a few notable exceptions, today's leaders treat stress and overwork as a badge of honor, brag about how little they sleep and how few vacation days they take, and have their reputations as workaholics carefully tended by publicists and corporate P.R. firms."[4] It is often difficult for others to be emotionally intelligent in such a milieu.

Group relations within the organization also can influence how much leaders use their emotional intelligence. As Annika Scholl, a psychologist at the Leibniz-Institut für Wissensmedien, in Tübingen, Germany, noted, people tend to be more sympathetic toward those who are in the same group.[5] This can apply to any kind of group, including a group based on race, gender, sexual orientation, occupation, religion, and so on. For instance, a male engineer may find it more difficult to empathize with female engineers than with another male engineer, which could lead to inaccurate and insensitive comments about the aptitude of females for math and science. The effect of intergroup relations on leaders' use of EI also applies to organizational groups such as marketing and engineering in a high-tech firm or English and chemistry departments in a university. Leaders, as members of these groups, may find it more difficult to use their emotional intelligence when dealing with people from other groups, especially if there has been a history of tension between the groups.[6]

THE IMPACT OF STRESS ON THE USE
OF EMOTIONAL INTELLIGENCE

Stressful work situations also can be an impediment to leaders' use of their EI: Insensitive, dictatorial leadership sometimes is a response to the pressures of the job. When stress and anxiety increase, leaders tend to clamp down. As their fear of failure increases, so does their need for control. Also, stressed-out leaders have less emotional energy for the extra time and effort sometimes required for emotionally intelligent leadership.

A number of writers have documented the relationship between stress and less emotionally intelligent behavior in leaders. Williams reviewed a large number of studies suggesting that leaders are more selfish and less responsive to other's needs when they feel threatened. She found that when they felt they were losing control or the respect of others, leaders are more likely to "lash out."[7] And Thompson has devoted a whole book to detailing how stress affects leaders' decision-making abilities as well as their sensitivity and effectiveness in handling interpersonal relations.[8]

Boyatzis and McKee have presented numerous case examples detailing how leaders' use of their EI declined when they encountered stressful situations.[9] There was the financial services executive who was no longer "cool, collected, and emotionally open" when he encountered a high level of stress due to turbulence in the industry. Another executive, who encountered high levels of stress when he was transferred to a particularly challenging position, became more rigid and paid less attention to relationships. He also became less aware of his own behavior, feelings, and impulses and had more difficulty in managing his emotions. Other leaders became less patient, less diplomatic, and less attuned to cultural messages. As a result, people stopped trusting them and did not want to be around them. When people are under stress, the brain shuts down nonessential neural circuits, leading to less openness, flexibility, and creativity.[10] And the negative emotions associated with stress are contagious.

A number of factors contribute to a person's stress response. Some have to do with individual personality, including one's emotional intelligence. However, factors in the social context also influence how much stress we experience and how it affects us.[11] Although EI can help us reduce stress, high levels of stress also can reduce the amount of EI available for managing it.[12]

SOURCES OF STRESS FOR LEADERS

Organizational leaders, like others, experience many common sources of stress in their jobs, including long hours, job insecurity and lack of work-life balance.[13] The pressure to achieve results, which contributes to many of the other stressors, is especially high for leaders, as are the costs for failing. When leaders are not able to deliver, they often must deal with the disappointment and anger of others. And even when they are able to meet expectations, for many the fear of failure never entirely goes away.

One of the most significant sources of organizational stress is a perceived lack of control and autonomy.[14] In one of the largest studies of work stress ever conducted, the researchers assessed the health status of a random sample of 8,504 full-time Swedish white-collar workers over a period of several years.[15] During the course of the study, 1,937 of the participants worked in companies that underwent reorganization. When the researchers looked more closely at the experiences of these workers, they found that some of them were allowed to have some influence over the reorganization process and gained increased task control as a result of it, while others had no influence over the process and ended up with less control in their jobs, providing a rare "experiment-in-nature."

When the researchers looked at the health status scores of the workers after the change, they found that those who gained control were significantly healthier.[16] For instance, 8.6% of the men who experienced a loss of control in their jobs showed signs of coronary heart disease, while only 3.4% of those who gained control showed signs. In other words, workers who had less control over their work situations after the reorganization were more than twice as likely to have signs of coronary heart disease as those who gained control. Absenteeism also was twice as high for those who lost control (10.7% vs. 5.0%), as was depression (27.8% vs. 13.7%). The changes were comparable for women.[17]

We often assume that leaders have more control than others. However, because leaders are *expected* to have more control, a perceived lack of control can be particularly stressful. And it is not just others who expect them to have the control necessary to make things happen; leaders expect it of themselves.

THE IMPACT OF THE JOB ON THE USE OF EMOTIONAL INTELLIGENCE

A job filled with boring and meaningless tasks also can discourage leaders from using their emotional intelligence. Having to get up every day and go to work in a job that feels insignificant and uninspiring can generate a level of chronic stress that may be even more damaging to one's health than periodic bouts of acute stress.[18] And like other sources of stress, a lack of meaningful and stimulating work can undermine a person's caring and commitment.

A rather dramatic example was a young lawyer whom one of us interviewed as a part of a study of professional burnout in new professionals.[19] Margaret W. had gone to a top law school and was on track for a prestigious job in a major law firm. However, she was dedicated to helping the poor and disadvantaged, and so she chose instead to work in a neighborhood legal aid office. To her dismay, she found that much of her daily work involved routine administrative duties that required little of the legal skills she had developed in law school. She also discovered that her efforts rarely made a difference for the people she represented:

> I spend more of my time on the phone than anything else . . . a lot of welfare and social security problems. . . . I also spend a lot of time doing routine things like name changes and guardianships. . . . A lot of times, there's nothing that's at all a legal question, but the person just doesn't know what's happening or doesn't know how to sit tight

and wait. . . . At first I was so happy that I got this job, I wasn't going to criticize anything at all. But recently I started getting sick of doing all of this real diddly shit and not getting into any big cases.[20]

After just 8 months in this job, Margaret had lost much of her idealism and compassion. She complained that many of her clients lied to her, and she confessed that she was seriously thinking of going to work for the prosecuting attorney's office so she could put some of them "behind bars where they belong."

We saw this same pattern in many of the other new professionals we studied. They began with high levels of idealism and compassion, but after many months of working in a boring, unstimulating job, which lacked meaning and utilized little of their professional training, they became less caring and committed. They still had their emotional intelligence, but they often did not use it.

When one's work situation does provide intellectual challenge and meaningful work experiences, one might be motivated to use more emotional intelligence. Another lawyer whom we interviewed, Jean C., had a background and aspirations that were similar to Margaret's. Jean also worked for legal aid. However, her job provided more opportunities to do interesting work that made a significant impact on the larger system. She worked in a special branch that specialized in reform work. Along with a small group of other dedicated lawyers, she handled class action lawsuits that had the potential to change the lives of thousands of people. And, unlike Margaret, Jean maintained the commitment and compassion she had when she began her career; in fact, it seemed to increase.

Other research, involving more standardized measures and larger samples, has confirmed what we found in our in-depth interviews with new professionals: People are more likely to use their emotional intelligence when their jobs are meaningful and stimulating. Perhaps the most striking example was one of the rare longitudinal studies of people's values and how they change over time. The researchers began with a sample of 694 men who were in their senior year of college. The students completed a set of questionnaires that assessed their work-related values at that time. Ten years later, the researchers were able to track down most of the original group, and 84% of them were willing to complete another set of questionnaires, including some that assessed the nature of the settings in which they had worked since college. The results showed that the men who worked in jobs with more challenge and opportunity for innovative thinking became more people-oriented.[21] Thus, the nature of the work that leaders do also influences how much emotional intelligence they are likely to use.

ENCOURAGING LEADERS TO USE EMOTIONAL INTELLIGENCE BY CHANGING THE CULTURE

An organizational culture that values emotional intelligence, monitors stress, and strives to make jobs meaningful can create a milieu in which leaders have the motivation and opportunities to use their EI. Organizations also can facilitate the development and use of the EI-based strategies we have presented in this book. And there are many organizations that have done so.

One example was American Express Financial Advisors (AEFA, now named Ameriprise), which developed a training program in "emotional competence" in 1992, 3 years before Daniel Goleman's bestseller on emotional intelligence appeared.[22] The effort began with research showing how financial advisors' emotional reactions sometimes adversely affected their performance. A training program then was designed to help them better identify and cope with the emotions associated with their work. After a rigorous evaluation study showed that advisors who went through the program actually generated more revenue for the company than a comparison group that received no training, it became a standard part of training for new advisors. Versions of the program also were created for the company's manager development program, and eventually there were versions for regional management sales teams and management teams in the corporate office. The development of the Emotional Competence program not only helped organizational leaders learn more emotionally intelligent ways of leading people but also helped make the company's culture more EI-friendly.

Another company that has sought to develop an EI-friendly culture is TDIndustries, a privately held construction firm in Dallas. According to a report in the *New York Times*,[23] the company "has embraced a principle known as 'servant leadership'" and "uses a number of techniques to ensure that its leaders work not to exploit workers but to enable them to flourish." Every year, for instance, "employees evaluate their supervisors. They are asked whether their manager treats them fairly, offers appropriate training, and includes them in their team. The feedback affects supervisors' salaries and promotions." Any manager who receives poor scores receives "extra adult supervision." The company, "which has appeared consistently on Fortune's annual list of the top 100 workplaces in the United States, *sees sensitive leadership as a matter of policy* [emphasis added]."

SPECIFIC STRATEGIES FOR ENCOURAGING THE USE OF EI

These model organizations, and others like them, encourage the use of emotional intelligence by their leaders in a number of ways. Some of these approaches target individuals and their jobs, while others help make the entire organization hospitable for the use of EI by its leaders. Organizations often go first to leadership training, and as we saw in the case of the Emotional Competence program, well-designed and well-implemented training programs can be effective.[24] However, as a strategy for helping individuals become more emotionally intelligent, formal training programs have some inherent limitations. Learners, for instance, sometimes find it difficult to apply what they learned in a training class back on the job. In fact, one estimate is that less than 10% of skills learned outside of the workplace actually get used when the learners return to the job.[25] The reasons are many. Time and work demands take leaders away from important practice that needs to happen in order to sharpen such skills. Participants also may have difficulty due to the dissonance between what they learned in class and how their organizations operate in the real world. And the fear of making mistakes in an era of intense scrutiny makes learners less willing to try something new.

BEYOND TRAINING: OTHER STRATEGIES
FOR ENCOURAGING THE USE OF EI

Fortunately, organizations can use several other approaches, in addition to training, to encourage their leaders to use the EI strategies. We already have seen how Cynthia's engineering firm instituted discussion groups as a follow-up to training with a focus on using emotional intelligence (see Chapter 9). The groups made a significant impact in part because of the way in which they were implemented. First, the company already had been working with an outside consulting group for more than a year to teach all the employees about emotional intelligence and how to use it in their jobs. Second, the initial training involved the top leadership group, and the first discussion group was made up of the top leaders. The groups eventually involved all the employees and met regularly. In addition, the groups were led by Cynthia and other members of the top leadership team, who received training and ongoing guidance from outside experts. As a result, the discussion groups not only helped individuals to use their EI in many different settings but also had a significant impact on the organizational culture.

Organizations also can promote the use of emotional intelligence by addressing some of the factors in a leader's job that contribute to stress. In a recent article in the *Harvard Business Review*, Eric Garton, a partner at Bain & Company, suggested that one of the most important sources of burnout is the lack of time for creative work.[26] And Daniel J. Levitin, a cognitive neuroscientist and professor of psychology at McGill University, noted that current research points to the value of taking breaks and letting the mind wander on a regular basis.[27] It not only promotes physical health but also leads to more meaningful activity. Thus, a simple but powerful way to reduce stress is to set aside time on a regular basis for reflection free of distractions.

New York Times columnist David Leonhardt has suggested a concrete way to set aside time for reflection: He carves out "an hour each week with no meetings, no phone calls, no email, no Twitter, no Facebook, no mobile alerts and no podcasts." He sets his phone to ring "only if my wife calls," and he keeps a pen and paper with him to jot down any interesting ideas that pop into his mind. The basic purpose is to reflect on information that is already in his mind rather than continue to collect new information.[28] Although any leader can do this on his or her own, organizations can encourage it and even create specific times when their leaders are expected to set aside everything else and give their brains some down time.

Organizations also could reduce stress and thus promote greater use of EI by helping to close the gap between their leaders' personal values and what they must do on their jobs. One way to do this is to make it possible for all leaders to develop new projects, programs, or functions that are particularly interesting and meaningful to them. These personal projects could be a small part of their job or they could be the whole job for a period of time. But whatever form it takes, it should represent a unique, personal way to experiment, to create, and to take a break from more routine activities—a way of making an impact and leaving one's mark on the world. And it should feel like the person's *own* program—something he or she can point to and say, "This is *my* program. I created it from scratch and it represents who I am and what I want to be."

A number of companies have used this strategy as a way to engage workers while also reaping the benefits of their projects. Those benefits sometimes can be enormous. Google was famous for its "20-percent policy," which allowed many of its employees to use up to 20% of their time to pursue their own pet projects. (One of the more spectacular outcomes was Gmail.) Google eventually discontinued the practice, but other companies, including LinkedIn, Apple, and Microsoft, have instituted similar programs. And it is not just tech companies that have used this strategy. According to one report, "Companies of all types, from investment banks to ad firms, are now known to be explicitly tolerant of side-entrepreneurship."[29]

Giving leaders time to pursue personal projects can help create a more hospitable climate for emotionally intelligent behavior. But the critical ingredient is to provide leaders with enough autonomy and support in their jobs so that they can feel that what they are doing has meaning—not just for the organization but for themselves and their teams.

In addition to innovative practices like discussion groups and personal projects, organizations also can promote the use of EI through some of their regular human resource management processes. On the most basic level, organizations can define every leader's role as including the emotionally intelligent management of their subordinates and then explicitly evaluate how well they perform this function, as TDIndustries has done.

Another human resource development process, career assessment and planning, can reduce some of the stress that undermines EI by helping leaders stay connected to their personal values as well as to organizational goals. In making job assignments, organizations could explicitly try to ensure that there is a good fit between what the leaders must do and their knowledge, abilities, and values. In addition, recruitment and selection could be designed so that there is a good fit between applicants' personal values and the requirements of the job to be filled. These HR practices would not guarantee that leaders use their emotional intelligence more, but they would reduce some of the obstacles, such as stress, boredom, and frustration, that discourage the leaders from doing so.[30]

Ultimately, however, these various strategies will fail unless the culture and top leadership of the organization actively support emotionally intelligent behavior. Top leaders need to use EI themselves in dealing with challenging situations, and the way they do it should be highlighted whenever possible in meetings, newsletters, training programs, and other media. The link between EI and the bottom line needs to be broadcast in every way possible.

NOTES

1. Lindebaum and Cassell (2012, p. 65).
2. Boyatzis and McKee (2005, p. 49).
3. Boyatzis and McKee (2005, p. 50).
4. Soojung-Kim Pang (2016). The quotation comes from a review of the book by Huffington (2016).
5. Scholl's comments appeared in an article by Hutson (2017).
6. Alderfer (2011).
7. Williams (2014).
8. Thompson (2010).
9. Boyatzis and McKee (2005, pp. 36–48).
10. Thompson (2010).
11. The classic work on this "transactional" view of stress is the book by Lazarus and Folkman (1984).
12. Wiens (2016, 2017) has shown particularly well how leaders' use of emotional and social competencies can help them to cope with stress.
13. There is a large body of research on workplace stress. A good summary can be found in Goh, Pfeffer, and Zenios (2016).
14. See, for example, Dickerson and Kemeny (2004).
15. Karasek (1990).
16. More specifically, the differences were statistically significant on 11 of 12 indicators for males and 4 of 12 indicators for females.
17. For instance, the prevalence of depression was 21.1% for women who ended up in jobs with greater control compared to 35.6% for those with less control.
18. See Sandler, Braver, and Gensheimer (2000).
19. Cherniss (1995).
20. Cherniss (1995, p. 26).
21. Mortimer and Lorence (1979). They also found that income reduced the salience of people-oriented values over time: When people's work provided higher income, they became less people-oriented. Unfortunately, organizational leaders, especially in large corporations, receive high levels of compensation for work that is not necessarily personally meaningful. See, for example, Ingoglia (2017).
22. The program is described in more detail in Cherniss and Adler (2000) and Cherniss and Caplan (2001).
23. Hutson (2017, p. BU11).
24. Information about some other well-designed, evidence-based programs can be found in Cherniss and Adler (2000).
25. See Schneider (2014).
26. Garton (2017).
27. Levitin (2014).

28. Leonhardt (2017). He learned the technique from former secretary of state George Schultz.
29. Subramanian (2013).
30. Executive coaching, with a focus on helping leaders to become more aware of their personal values and to use that awareness to make their work more meaningful, is another approach. See the recent book by Boyatzis, Smith, and Van Oosten (2019) for an excellent discussion of to accomplish this.

12

Taking Charge

W e all have faced situations like the ones described in this book, and it is at those times that the nine strategies presented here can help us to meet those challenges and capitalize on those opportunities. What made the outstanding leaders in our study so effective was not just having emotional intelligence. It was the way in which they used it, and that usually involved one or more of those EI strategies.

SOME GUIDING PRINCIPLES FOR USING THE EI STRATEGIES

Throughout this book we have provided activities that you can use to help you develop and apply each of the EI strategies. As you engage in these activities and then use the strategies in your work life (and personal life, too, if you wish), here are a few guiding principles to keep in mind.

Your Beliefs About Emotions and Feelings Make a Critical Difference. It was not just the strategies that made the difference in the critical situations these leaders described. They used those strategies effectively because they believed that, like it or not, emotions inevitably play an important role in the workplace. This understanding led them to be more open to and aware of their own emotions and those of others, and to channel those emotions in positive ways. They recognized that emotions are not just noise or an obstacle to be pushed out of the way; rather, they often provide valuable information and motivate people to make an extra effort. In short, the leaders seemed to respect emotions and seek to understand and use them. Cynthia, the CEO of a large engineering firm, perhaps said it best. At one point near the end of our interview, we commented that emotions seem to be a "big part of the job," to which she emphatically replied, "It *is* the job—the biggest part of the job and the hardest part of the job is managing the emotional element."

To use the nine EI strategies in a way that helps us to be better leaders, we need to agree with the proposition that emotions inevitably occur at work. People cannot just set them aside when they begin their workday. And so it is better to pay attention to emotions and figure out positive ways to use them.

Using the EI Strategies Sometimes Takes a Little Extra Time, but It's Worth It. As you begin to use these strategies, it may seem that they slow you down. And it is true that doing things in a more emotionally intelligent way sometimes takes extra time and effort. But it is a good investment.

When Cynthia talked about how she handled the layoffs at her company during the Great Recession of 2008, she acknowledged that doing things in an emotionally intelligent way took extra time. But looking at the process in retrospect, she was convinced it was worth it. As she noted during our interview, "It would have taken more time to try to jam something down, and the cleanup would have been bad."

Not Every EI Strategy Will Work in Every Situation. An important part of emotional intelligence is knowing what strategies will work best at any point in time. Emotionally intelligent leaders do not depend on one particular strategy; as we saw in Chapter 10, they are versatile at switching and mixing them. As the emotions researcher Stefan G. Hofmann noted, "The most emotionally skilled among us are not wedded to any one strategy."[1]

You Often Must Use an EI Strategy Repeatedly for It to Have a Meaningful Impact. Using a strategy once to deal with a situation, no matter how effective it may be, will probably not have a significant, lasting impact by itself. One of the most important tasks of any leader is to create a positive emotional climate, and that involves acting in a certain way in many situations over sustained periods of time. For example, when Jonathan, a vice president in a health care products company, tried to help Manny, an abusive but valuable executive, to behave with more emotional intelligence, he initially met with considerable resistance (Chapter 9). Manny saw Jonathan as the enemy, not a source of support. Eventually, Manny was willing to learn from Jonathan how to work in a more emotionally intelligent way. But Jonathan first had to create a more positive relationship with Manny, and that took repeated use of several EI strategies over a considerable period of time.

Be Prepared to Make Mistakes, and Don't Be Too Discouraged When You Do. Many of the leaders we studied told us about mistakes they had made during their careers, and we were struck by how they responded to those situations: They did not give up. Sometimes they needed a bit of time to recover emotionally, but they soon focused on what they could learn from the mistakes and then tried another approach.

One thing that helped them to persist and learn from their mistakes was that they avoided the trap of perfectionism. They did not expect that they would always be right; they were aware that they had limitations and that they would inevitably make mistakes. They also had confidence that no matter how big the mistake seemed, things would work out OK in the end.

Harold, the successful CEO of a large supermarket chain, was one of those leaders who explicitly talked about the inevitability of making mistakes. One of those mistakes involved Harold's predecessor, who, just before he left, asked Harold to promote someone who "shouldn't have been promoted." Harold did so against his better judgment to give his predecessor "peace of mind as he left for Florida." The result was not good. As he said, "It was a bombshell because people hated this woman. Then the whole thing imploded and I had to terminate her, which was very painful for her and very painful for me." Harold made some other mistakes during his first year or so on the job. But he did not expect to be perfect, and he learned from those mistakes.

He still had high expectations for himself, and he still felt bad when he made a mistake. But he recognized that it was inevitable he would do so. He knew that the idea of a "flawless leader" is a myth.[2] He avoided the trap of perfectionism, and so he was able to persevere and move on when he made a mistake.[3] That made it easier for Harold to look at his mistakes and learn from them.

WHAT IF AN ORGANIZATION IS NOT EI-FRIENDLY?

As we noted in Chapter 11, organizations sometimes discourage leaders from using their emotional intelligence. However, our research suggests that if leaders find themselves in such an organization, they can some-times use their emotional intelligence to work around it. A good example was Karen, the food services manager who discovered that one of her employees had filed a false report with the government alleging that their company had violated some safety regulations (see Chapter 10). Once Karen "unofficially" discovered who the employee was, she had to report it to her superiors. Because the employee "wasn't a particular favorite of the higher-ups," Karen knew that they would want her to fire the employee immediately. But Karen wanted to use a more emotionally intelligent ap-proach. She recalled: "When I told my superiors that I thought I knew who the employee was, they said, 'Fire her, go after her!' And I said, 'We can't do that; we can't even confront her with the fact that there was a complaint.' . . . So I got the trust of my superiors to let me handle this with the person in an appropriate way." After Karen talked with the em-ployee and discovered that the employee's frustration, anger, and sadness over her husband's recently diagnosed cancer had led to her filing the false charges, Karen had to go back to her superiors and report on it. They were still not sympathetic. They said, "Well that's a shame, but let's find a way to get rid of her." Karen replied, "No, we're not going to do that. We're going to put her in a better place and hopefully she'll return to the productive employee that she was before." Looking back, Karen said, "It was going against my superiors' wishes, but they were going off the handle, and we couldn't do what they wanted to do anyway."

When we asked Karen for more details on how she was able to secure her superiors' support, she said: "Fortunately, I had the support of corporate human resources. Anticipating upper management's negative reaction, I had told HR about the situation first. So when I said to my superiors, "We can't do that," I knew they were going to hear the same thing from HR. So I had to prepare myself by going to HR first and getting them behind me before I talked to people I knew were going to be hostile." In this incident, Karen used her knowledge of the rules and procedures regarding labor relations, as well as some help from her contacts in HR, to overcome her superiors' opposition to using a more emotionally intelligent approach.[4]

When possible, it is usually a good idea for leaders to respect and adhere to the prevailing culture in order to build up credibility and trust. This credibility will then enable leaders to sometimes act in ways that may be countercultural.[5] One of the leaders in our study who demonstrated how this works was Julia, a corporate vice president for human resources in a multinational company. In Chapter 7 we described how she conducted a team-building session for a group of sales vice presidents who had worked together well in the past but were no longer supporting each other. What she did, and the way she did it, were highly unusual for the company: "This was a very data-driven company. No one ever talked about their feelings. But I wanted to appeal to people's emotions. The problem wasn't about sales numbers and it wasn't about charts." So Julia began the session by having the team members sit in a circle without a table in front of them, and she asked, "How does it feel to be on this team?"

Looking back on the session, Julia acknowledged that "it was a really risky thing to do because I went to a group of people who never talked about their feelings. I put my chair right in the middle of the room like Oprah, and I could see everyone thinking, 'Where is she going with this!' So it was risky." Even having the team sit in a circle was viewed as a threatening departure from the norm.

However, Julia was allowed to do what she did because she had been working with the group as their designated HR person for some time, and she regularly sat in on their meetings. So the team had a chance to get to know Julia and see that she usually respected their norms. As a result, they had come to trust her. The team members' boss, who was the head of sales for the whole company, also trusted Julia. He had been talking with her for some time about what was happening with the team and how "things were starting to come unglued." Julia said, "Normally I would run anything I planned to do past him first by showing him the PowerPoints or whatever, but this time I said to him, 'Just trust me on this one.' And he did."

Julia's intervention with the team was effective, but she never would have been able to do it unless she had been viewed as a responsible and conscientious professional. Her reputation as someone who respected the company's culture enabled her to do something that dramatically departed from some of its norms on this one occasion.[6]

SOME GUIDELINES FOR SECURING ORGANIZATIONAL SUPPORT

These examples, along with others that we heard about, point to three guidelines that leaders can follow to secure organizational support for emotionally intelligent behavior. First, use your emotional and social competence to develop positive relationships with key decision makers and members of powerful groups so that you are viewed as a loyal, positive, and trustworthy member of the organization. Second, use your EI to manage the emotions that might be stirred up, such as righteous indignation or fear of losing the esteem of others, as you take the initiative and challenge the system. And third, learn the relevant rules and regulations so that you can use them for added leverage. Seek the help of knowledge-able others, such as people in HR, if necessary.

CONCLUSION

In this book we have suggested that emotional intelligence can play an important role when leaders confront critical challenges and opportunities. However, what matters most is how they *use* their emotional intelligence. Skill in detecting how someone is feeling based on their nonverbal facial expressions is useful, but it is not enough. Even a capacity to empathize with others will be of limited value unless one knows how to use that empathy to support and influence others, and the social context supports doing so. We have presented nine strategies, based on emotional intelligence, that a group of outstanding leaders used in dealing with critical situations. They are strategies that others can use as well. And we believe that doing so will ultimately result in healthier, happier, and more effective individuals *and* organizations.

NOTES

1. The quotation comes from Carey (2010).
2. For more on the "myth of the flawless leader," see Ancona, Malone, Orlikowski, and Senge (2007).
3. Amy Guttman, the president of the University of Pennsylvania, observed, "Perfection is highly overrated. Do not strive for perfection. If you do, you won't take risks" (quoted in Bryant, 2011, June 19).
4. As we noted in the introduction, this kind of "organizational awareness" is one of the 12 emotional and social competencies in Boyatzis and Goleman's model.
5. This idea is based on the concept of *idiosyncrasy credits*, first articulated by Hollander (1958). The basic notion is that whenever group members conform to a group's expectations, they earn an idiosyncrasy credit, and when they violate an expectation, they lose a credit. When people have a positive balance of these credits, they can act in idiosyncratic ways. However, each time they do so they reduce their balance.
6. For another example of how a leader assiduously showed respect for his company's culture to gain the credibility and trust he needed to make major changes, see Harold's story in Chapter 5.

Leaders Who Participated in the Research

Name[1]	Organizational Setting
Aaron	CEO of a construction company
Amy	Nursery school director
Bruce	Superintendent of a suburban school district
Charles	Family business owner
Clarence	District manager for a state child protective services agency
Cynthia	CEO of an engineering firm
Diane	Head of corporate leadership training for a large hotel chain
Doreen	Nursery school director
Dorothy	Executive director of a small, nonprofit social service agency
Harold	CEO of a large supermarket chain
James	Senior vice president in a large consulting practice
Jeffrey	President of a private university
Jonathan	Vice president for human resources in a health care device manufacturing company
Julia	Vice president for corporate human resources in a large pharmaceutical company
Karen	District manager in a large, industrial food services company
Linda	Director and vice president of product development for a large clothing company

Martha	Founder and executive director of a small, nonprofit human service agency
Mary	Corporate vice president of human resources for a large chemicals and materials firm
Michael	President of an agricultural products company
Ronald	Principal of a private, religiously affiliated high school
Ruth	Director of wholesale planning and operations for a large clothing company
Sam	Executive director of a large, residential health care facility
Sondra	District manager for a state's child protective services agency
Tom	COO of a large steel company
Yolanda	Director of leadership development for a large clothing company

[1] All names are pseudonyms.

Research Method

This book was based on a study of how outstanding organizational leaders think about and use emotion in critical situations. Data came primarily from behavioral event interviews with 25 leaders from a variety of settings. The goal was to explore how the leaders actually used and managed emotions in their day-to-day work.

The leaders came from a range of organizations, including large pharmaceutical and steel companies, medium-size engineering and architectural consulting firms, and family-owned businesses. They also came from suburban school systems; private nursery schools; large state welfare agencies; and small, nonprofit, community-based social service programs. The leaders included mid-level managers, senior-level executives, and CEOs. Just over half (13) were women. In addition, two were African American, one was Asian American, and the rest were White. A list of the leaders' pseudonyms, job titles, and work settings can be found in Appendix A.

The leaders were selected based on nominations by management consultants, executive coaches, and other leaders who knew them well. We asked the nominators to suggest leaders who were "effective and seem to use and manage emotions especially well." Our rationale for selecting the leaders in this way is that we wanted a sample of individuals who were likely to use emotional intelligence in many situations. Five leaders who were nominated chose not to participate in the research (an 83% positive response rate).

The interviews lasted from 45 to 90 minutes and were audio recorded with the leaders' consent. Twenty were done in person and the other five by phone. The authors conducted 20 of the interviews; two doctoral students in psychology,[1] who were trained and supervised by the first author (Cherniss), conducted the remaining five interviews.

The interviews were based on the behavioral event method, which was adapted from the "critical incident" technique.[2] After collecting some information about the leader's work history and current job, the interviewer said, "Now I'd like you to take a minute to think of two or three recent incidents in which you managed or used emotion—yours and others—to deal with a problem or achieve a goal (pause). . . . OK, can you describe it to me?" In most cases, the interviewers sent this lead-off question to the participants ahead of time so that they would have a chance to think about it. After the leader described the incident, and the interviewer asked questions to fill in any gaps in the story, the interviewer used probes to get more information on how the leader may have used each of the core EI abilities: (a) identifying emotions—own and others, (b) expressing emotion, (c) using emotions to facilitate thought, (d) understanding emotions (i.e., insight about why people reacted as they did), (e) managing one's own emotions, and (f) managing others' emotions. For example, after the leader had described an incident, the interviewer might ask, "Do you recall how you were feeling when the other person did x?" and then might follow up with, "How do you think you expressed those feelings?" and "What impact did that seem to have?"

Fifteen of the interviews were fully transcribed; for the other 10, only segments relating to the primary research questions were transcribed and the rest of the interview was summarized. In the first phase of the research, we read through the transcripts and summaries several times and identified themes related to how the leaders used the core emotional intelligence abilities to deal with the incidents. We then developed a working code book based on the themes.[3] One of the authors (Cherniss) then went back over the transcripts, marked specific segments that demonstrated one or more themes, and coded them. Then the other author (Roche) independently coded the incidents for the themes. We calculated the inter-rater agreement for each theme using the following formula for ordinal or nominal data: [4]

$$\frac{2 \times \left(\text{no. of times both coder A and coder B saw theme present}\right)}{\left(\text{no. of times coder A saw it present } + \text{ no. of times coder B saw it present}\right)}$$

Six of the themes had reliability coefficients of .75 or higher. The two raters then discussed the incidents on which there was disagreement and decided consensually how to code them.

The final phase involved selecting the themes that seemed most significant and meaningful. "Meaningfulness" was determined by how often a theme appeared in an incident, how closely it related to the primary research question, and how novel it seemed to be as a discovery. For instance, one theme was "Used a specific coping strategy." Although this theme appeared relatively frequently, it was not selected among the final set because it seemed too general and did not seem to be particularly novel or helpful.

As we considered the themes that emerged from our analysis, we realized that they could be conceptualized as strategies that the leaders used for working with emotions effectively. This framework became the basis for the book.

NOTES

1. Cassia Mosdell and Alexandra Glovinsky.
2. The critical incident technique was first described by Flanagan (1954). For more information about the method, see Boyatzis (1997); Janz (1982); Motowidlo et al. (1992); Ronan and Latham (1974).
3. We used the approach suggested by Boyatzis (1997).
4. The formula was recommended by Boyatzis (1997, p. 155).

Links Between Emotional Intelligence Strategies,
Abilities, and Competencies

The following table shows how the nine strategies presented in this book are linked to specific emotional intelligence abilities and emotional and social competencies. The emotional intelligence abilities are based on Mayer and Salovey's model (Mayer, Salovey, Caruso, & Cherkasskiy, 2011), and the emotional and social competencies are based on the work of Boyatzis and Goleman (Boyatzis, 2009). Note that the assignment of abilities and competencies to strategies reflects the authors' views only.

STRATEGY	EMOTIONAL INTELLIGENCE ABILITIES	EMOTIONAL AND SOCIAL COMPETENCIES
1. Monitor the emotional climate.	• Emotion perception • Emotion understanding	• Empathy • Organizational awareness
2. Express your feelings to motivate others.	• Emotion perception • Facilitating thought	• Inspirational leadership • Influence
3. Consider how your own behavior influences others' emotions.	• Emotion understanding	• Emotional self-awareness • Empathy • Organizational awareness

4. Put yourself in others' shoes.	• Emotion understanding • Emotion perception	• Emotional self-awareness • Empathy • Organizational awareness
5. Decipher the underlying emotional dynamics of a situation.	• Emotion understanding	• Empathy • Organizational awareness
6. Reframe how you think about the situation.	• Emotion management	• Emotional self-control • Positive outlook • Adaptability • Empathy • Organizational awareness
7. Create optimal interpersonal boundaries.	• Emotion management • Emotion understanding	• Emotional self-awareness • Emotional self-control • Empathy • Organizational awareness
8. Seek out others for help in managing emotions.	• Emotion management	• Emotional self-awareness • Emotional self-control • Adaptability • Teamwork
9. Help others develop their EI abilities.	• Emotion management • Emotion understanding • Facilitating thought	• Empathy • Organizational awareness • Coach and mentor • Teamwork

ACKNOWLEDGMENTS

First, we would like to thank the 25 leaders who contributed their time and wisdom to this endeavor. Unfortunately, we cannot name them because of our promise of confidentiality, but this book would not have been possible without the interviews they graciously gave us. We learned an enormous amount from each of them, and we are now pleased to be able to share much of what we learned with others.

We could not have learned anything from those outstanding leaders without several people who helped us identify them. They include Kathy Cavallo, Ted Freeman, Monica Knopf, Philip Brown, Cassia Mosdell, and Alexi Glovinsky. We are grateful for their invaluable help.

We also would like to acknowledge the 100-plus members of the Consortium for Research on Emotional Intelligence in Organizations (CREIO). Its members include many of the leading scholars and practitioners in the field, and it has been a major source of research and practical wisdom in the field of emotional intelligence for more than 20 years. We are especially grateful for the contributions of Daniel Goleman, the founder and co-chair, as well as those of the founding and core members: Richard Boyatzis, Robert Caplan, Stéphane Côté, Vanessa Druskat, Hillary Anger Elfenbein, Marilyn Gowing, Ronald Humphrey, Kathy Kram, Richard Price, Mary Ann Re, Helen Riess, Lyle Spencer Jr., Scott Taylor, and Roger Weissberg. Several staff members also have contributed in important and unique ways. They include Robert Emmerling, Fatos Kusari, Melissa Extein, and Mitchel Adler. (One of us, Cornelia Roche, was also an early staff member.)

We also want to thank the many organizations that have supported CREIO's work over the years. The Fetzer Institute provided the initial funding starting in 1996. Other organizations that have helped since then are the US Office of Personnel Management, Johnson & Johnson, Egon Zehnder International, the Hay Group (now part of Korn Ferry), think2perform, Fifth Third Bank, Constellation/MMIC, Ameriprise, United Healthcare, Hindustan Petroleum, Amcor, Schlumberger, Spencer Stuart, Wawa, Cigna, MD Anderson Cancer Center, and Genos International. In addition to their financial support, those organizations also sent people who made many contributions to the intellectual work of our group at our semiannual meetings and beyond. They include Claudio Fernández-Aráoz, Matthew Mangino, Doug Lennick, Rick Aberman, Lauris Woolford, Ashis Sen, Laurie Drill-Mellum, Steve Freeman, Donna Gregory, Fabio Sala, Steve Kelner, Ruth Malloy, Signe Spencer, Steve Wolff, and Ben Palmer.

We have also benefited greatly from the many teachers and colleagues at Rutgers University's Graduate School of Applied and Professional Psychology (GSAPP) who created such a stimulating and supportive environment for our work. We especially acknowledge the contributions of Clayton P. Alderfer, Ruth Orenstein, Michele Ballet, Kathy Cavallo, and Christine Truhe in the Organizational Psychology doctoral program. Other GSAPP faculty who were especially supportive include Daniel Fishman, Susan Forman, Charlie Maher, Ken Schneider, John Kalafat, Sandra Harris, and Stanley Messer. We also appreciate the administrative staff members at GSAPP for the many ways they assisted with our efforts. They include Ruth Schulman, Jennifer Leon, Lew Gantwerk, Kathy McLean, Sylvia Kriger, Julie Skorny, Diane Crino, Thilda Coyman, and Maryhelen Dzuban.

A number of people read parts of the manuscript and provided invaluable feedback. We are particularly thankful for their help. They include Dennis N. T. Perkins, Amanda Rose, Kevin Engholm, Matt and Diane

Feldman, Robert Shaw, and Bradley Marcus. We also would like to thank Marilee Adams for her guidance at several points during the project.

We especially appreciate the many contributions of Deborah Cherniss. She not only devoted many hours to editing the manuscript at numerous times during the writing process but also provided unconditional love and support for Cary, which made the whole process both less difficult and less lonely. There is a good reason why so many of Cary's books, including this one, have been dedicated to her!

Finally, we thank the rest of our families for their love, warmth, and support.

Adams, M. (2009). *Change your questions, change your life: 10 powerful tools for life and work* (2nd ed.). San Francisco, CA: Berrett-Koehler.

Alderfer, C. P. (1980). Consulting to underbounded systems. In C. P. Alderfer & C. Cooper (Eds.), *Advances in experiential social processes* (Vol. 2, pp. 267–295). New York, NY: Wiley.

Alderfer, C. P. (2011). *The practice of organizational diagnosis: Theory and methods.* New York, NY: Oxford University Press.

Ancona, D., Malone, T. W., Orlikowski, W. J., & Senge, P. M. (2007, February). In praise of the incomplete leader. *Harvard Business Review.* Retrieved from https://hbr.org/product/in-praise-of-the-incomplete-leader/R0702E-PDF-ENG

Antonakis, J., Ashkanasy, N. M., & Dasborough, M. T. (2009). Does leadership need emotional intelligence? *Leadership Quarterly, 20,* 247–261.

Ashforth, B. E., & Humphrey, R. H. (1993). Emotional labor in service roles: The influence of identity. *Academy of Management Review, 18,* 88–115.

Athanasopoulou, A., & Dopson, S. (2018). A systematic review of executive coaching outcomes: Is it the journey or the destination that matters the most? *Leadership Quarterly, 29,* 70–88. doi:https://doi.org/10.1016/j.leaqua.2017.11.004

Bar-On, R. (2000). Emotional and social intelligence: Insights from the Emotional Quotient Inventory. In R. Bar-On & J. Parker (Eds.), *Handbook of emotional intelligence* (pp. 363–388). San Francisco, CA: Jossey-Bass.

Bar-On, R., Handley, R., & Fund, S. (2005). The impact of emotional intelligence on performance. In V. Druskat, F. Sala, & G. Mount (Eds.), *Linking emotional intelligence and performance at work: Current research evidence* (pp. 3–20). Mahwah, NJ: Erlbaum.

Barrett, L. F., & Salovey, P. (2002). Introduction. In L. F. Barrett & P. Salovey (Eds.), *The wisdom in feeling: Psychological processes in emotional intelligence* (pp. 1–8). New York, NY: Guilford Press.

Barsade, S. G. (2002). The ripple effect: Emotional contagion and its influence on group behavior. *Administrative Science Quarterly, 47*, 644–675.

Bass, B. M. (1981). *Stogdill's handbook of leadership* (2nd ed.). New York, NY: Free Press.

Bass, B. M. (2002). Cognitive, social, and emotional intelligence of transformational leaders. In R. E. Riggio, S. E. Murphy, & F. J. Pirozzolo (Eds.), *Multiple intelligences and leadership* (pp. 105–118). Mahwah, NJ: Erlbaum.

Bennis, W., & Shepard, H. (1956). A theory of group development. *Human Relations, 9*, 415–437.

Bennis, W. G., & Nanus, B. (2003). *Leaders: Strategies for taking charge* (2nd ed.). New York, NY: Harper and Row.

Bhalerao, H., & Kumar, S. (2016). Role of emotional intelligence in leaders on the commitment level of employees: A study in information technology and the manufacturing sector in India. *Business Perspectives and Research, 4*, 41–53. doi:10.1177/2278533715605434

Bono, J. E., & Ilies, R. (2006). Charisma, positive emotions, and mood contagion. *Leadership Quarterly, 17*, 317–334.

Boyatzis, R. E. (1997). *Transforming qualitative information: Thematic analysis and code development*. Thousand Oaks, CA: Sage.

Boyatzis, R. E. (1982). *The competent manager: A model for effective performance*. New York, NY: Wiley.

Boyatzis, R. E. (2007). Developing emotional intelligence through coaching for leadership, professional, and occupational excellence. In R. Bar-On, J. G. Maree, & M. J. Elias (Eds.), *Educating people to be emotionally intelligent* (pp. 155–168). New York, NY: Praeger.

Boyatzis, R. E. (2009). Competencies as a behavioral approach to emotional intelligence. *Journal of Management Development, 28*, 749–770.

Boyatzis, R. E., & McKee, A. (2005). *Resonant leadership*. Boston, MA: Harvard Business School Press.

Boyatzis, R. E., Smith, M., & Van Oosten, E. (2019). *Helping people change: Coaching with compassion for lifelong learning and growth*. Boston, MA: Harvard Review Press.

Bozer, G., & Jones, R. J. (2018). Understanding the factors that determine workplace coaching effectiveness: A systematic literature review. *European Journal of Work and Organizational Psychology, 27*, 342–361. doi:10.1080/1359432X.2018.1446946

Brody, J. E. (2017, March 28). Positive emotions may extend life. *New York Times*, p. D5.

Bryant, A. (2010, August 22). Memo to self: Don't take it personally. *New York Times*, p. BU2.

Bryant, A. (2010, August 25). Team insights? Just use your peripheral vision. *New York Times*, p. BU2.

Bryant, A. (2011, January 16). Say anything, but phrase it the right way. *New York Times*, BU2.

Bryant, A. (2011, March 13). The quest to build a better boss. *New York Times*, pp. BU1, 7.

Bryant, A. (2011, June 19). Welcoming the wild ideas of the week. *New York Times*, p. BU2.

Bryant, A. (2011, July 7). Looking ahead behind the ivy: The new dean of Harvard Business School, on leadership and character. *New York Times*, Education Life Supplement, 14.

Burns, J. M. (1978). *Leadership*. New York, NY: Harper and Row.

Bushman, B. J. (2002). Does venting anger feed or extinguish the flame? Catharsis, rumination, distraction, anger and aggressive responding. *Personality and Social Psychology Bulletin, 28*, 724–731.

Carey, B. (2010, July 6). The benefits of blowing your top. *New York Times*, p. D1.

Caruso, D. R., & Salovey, P. (2004). *The emotionally intelligent manager: How to develop and use the four key emotional skills of leadership*. San Francisco, CA: Jossey-Bass.

Cherniss, C. (1986). Different ways of thinking about burnout. In E. Seidman & J. Rappaport (Eds.), *Redefining social problems* (pp. 217–229). New York, NY: Plenum.

Cherniss, C. (1995). *Beyond burnout: Helping teachers, nurses, therapists, and lawyers overcome stress and disillusionment*. New York, NY: Routledge.

Cherniss, C. (2006). *School change and the MicroSociety program*. Thousand Oaks, CA: Corwin Press.

Cherniss, C., & Adler, M. (2000). *Promoting emotional intelligence in organizations*. Alexandria, VA: American Society for Training and Development.

Cherniss, C., & Caplan, R. D. (2001). Implementing emotional intelligence programs in organizations. In C. Cherniss & D. Goleman (Eds.), *The emotionally intelligent workplace* (pp. 286–304). San Francisco, CA: Jossey-Bass.

Chernow, R. (2010). *Washington: A life*. New York, NY: Penguin.

Cohn, M. A., Pietrucha, M. E., Saslow, L. R., Hult, J. R., & Moskowitz, J. T. (2014). An online positive affect skills intervention reduces depression in adults with type 2 diabetes. *Journal of Positive Psychology, 9*, 523–534. doi:10.1080/17439760.2014.920410

Cooper, C. L., & Cartwright, S. (2001). Organizational management of stress and destructive emotions at work. In R. L. Payne & C. L. Cooper (Eds.), *Emotions at work: Theory, research and applications for management* (pp. 269–280). Chichester, England: Wiley.

Côté, S. (2013, December). Emotional intelligence: Recent theoretical advances and research findings. Presentation at the fall meeting of the Consortium for Research on Emotional Intelligence (CREIO). Boston, MA.

Credé, M., Tynan, M. C., & Harms, P. D. (2017). Much ado about grit: A meta-analytic synthesis of the grit literature. *Journal of Personality and Social Psychology, 113*, 492–511. doi:http://dx.doi.org/10.1037/pspp0000102

Darwin, C. (1872). *The expression of the emotions in man and animals*. Chicago: University of Chicago Press.

Dattner, B., & Dahl, D. (2011). *The blame game*. New York, NY: Free Press.

Davis, M. H. (1983). Measuring individual differences in empathy: Evidence for a multidimensional approach. *Journal of Personality and Social Psychology, 44*, 113–126.

Decety, J., & Jackson, P. L. (2004). The functional architecture of human empathy. *Behavioral and Cognitive Neuroscience Reviews, 3*, 71–100.

Dickerson, S. S., & Kemeny, M. (2004). Acute stressors and cortisol responses: A theoretical integration and synthesis of laboratory research. *Psychological Bulletin, 130*, 355–391.

Dilworth, L., & Boshyk, Y. (Eds.). (2010). *Action learning and its applications*. London, England: Palgrave Macmillan UK.

Duckworth, A. L., & Seligman, M. E. P. (2005). Self-discipline outdoes IQ in predicting academic performance of adolescents. *Psychological Science, 16*, 939–944.

Edmondson, A. (1999). Psychological safety and learning behavior in work teams. *Administrative Science Quarterly, 44*, 350–383.

English, T., John, O. P., Srivastava, S., & Gross, J. J. (2012). Emotion regulation and peer-related social functioning: A 4-year longitudinal study. *Journal of Research in Personality, 46*, 780–784.

Epictetus. (2008). *Discourses and selected writings* (R. Dobbin, Trans.). London, England: Penguin.

Erskine, L. (2012). Defining relational distance for today's leaders. *International Journal of Leadership Studies, 7*, 96–113.

Fiedler, F. E. (2002). The curious role of cognitive resources in leadership. In R. E. Riggio, S. E. Murphy, & F. J. Pirozzolo (Eds.), *Multiple intelligences and leadership* (pp. 91–104). Mahwah, NJ: Erlbaum.

Flanagan, J. C. (1954). The critical incident technique. *Psychological Bulletin, 51*, 327–358. doi:10.1037/h0061470

Folkman,'S., & Moskowitz, J. T. (2000). Stress, positive emotion, and coping. *Current Directions in Psychological Science, 9*, 115–118. doi:10.1111/1467-8721.00073.

French, J. R. P., & Raven, B. (1959). The bases of social power. In D. Cartwright (Ed.), *Studies in social power* (pp. 150–167). Ann Arbor: University of Michigan Press.

Friedman, S. D. (Ed.). (1987). *Leadership succession*. New Brunswick, NJ: Transaction Books.

Garton, E. (2017, April 6). Employee burnout is a problem with the company, not the person. *Harvard Business Review*. Retrieved from https://hbr.org/2017/04/employee-burnout-is-a-problem-with-the-company-not-the-person

Geddes, D., & Callister, R. R. (2007). Crossing the line(s): A dual threshold model of expressing anger in organizations. *Academy of Management Review, 32*, 721–746.

George, J. M. (2000). Emotions and leadership: The role of emotional intelligence. *Human Relations, 53*, 1027–1055.

Goh, J., Pfeffer, J., & Zenios, S. A. (2016). The relationship between workplace stressors and mortality and health costs in the United States. *Management Science, 62*, 608–628. doi:10.1287/mnsc.2014.2015

Goleman, D. (1995). *Emotional intelligence*. New York, NY: Bantam.

Goleman, D. (1998). *Working with emotional intelligence*. New York, NY: Bantam.

Goleman, D. (2001). An EI-based theory of performance. In C. Cherniss & D. Goleman (Eds.), *The emotionally intelligent workplace: How to select for, measure, and improve emotional intelligence in individuals, groups, and organizations* (pp. 27–44). San Francisco, CA: Jossey-Bass.

Goleman, D. (2013). *Focus: The hidden driver of excellence*. New York, NY: Harper.

Goleman, D., Boyatzis, R., & McKee, A. (2002). *Primal leadership: Realizing the power of emotional intelligence*. Boston, MA: Harvard Business School Press.

Goodwin, D. K. (2013). *The bully pulpit: Theodore Roosevelt, William Howard Taft, and the golden age of journalism*. New York, NY: Simon and Schuster.

Gooty, J., Connelly, S., Griffith, J., & Gupta, A. (2010). Leadership, affect and emotions: A state of the science review. *Leadership Quarterly, 21,* 979–1004. doi:http://dx.doi.org/10.1016/j.leaqua.2010.10.005

Gottman, J. M. (1994). *What predicts divorce? The relationship between marital processes and marital outcomes.* Hillsdale, NJ: Erlbaum.

Hackman, J. R., & Wageman, R. (2005). A theory of team coaching. *Academy of Management Review, 30,* 269–287.

Hackman, J. R., & Wageman, R. (2007). Asking the right questions about leadership. *American Psychologist, 62,* 43–47.

Harms, P. D., & Credé, M. (2010). Remaining issues in emotional intelligence research: Construct overlap, method artifacts, and lack of incremental validity. *Industrial and Organizational Psychology: Perspectives on Science and Practice, 3,* 154–158.

Hess, U. (2014). Anger is a positive emotion. In W. G. Parrott (Ed.), *The positive side of negative emotions* (pp. 55–75). New York, NY: Guilford Press.

Hochschild, A. R. (1983). *The managed heart: Commercialization of human feeling.* Berkeley: University of California Press.

Hollander, E. (1958). Conformity, status, and idiosyncrasy credit. *Psychological Review, 65,* 117–127. doi:10.1037/h0042501. PMID 13542706.

Hopkins, M. M., & Bilmoria, D. (2008). Social and emotional competencies predicting success for male and female executives. *Journal of Management Development, 27,* 13–35.

Huffington, A. (2016, December 18). The rest of your life. *New York Times Book Review,* p. BR10.

Humphrey, R. H. (2012). How do leaders use emotional labor? *Journal of Organizational Behavior, 33,* 740–744.

Hutson, M. (2017, May 21). When power doesn't corrupt. *New York Times,* p. BU11.

Ingoglia, R. (2017, July 4). Independence Day idea: Life, liberty and the pursuit of a meaningful job. *NJ Star-Ledger Opinion.* https://www.nj.com/opinion/2017/07/life_liberty_and_the_pursuit_of_a_meaningful_job_o.html

Janz, T. (1982). Initial comparisons of patterned behavior description interviews versus unstructured interviews. *Journal of Applied Psychology, 67,* 577–580.

Jones, E. E., & Harris, V. A. (1967). The attribution of attitudes. *Journal of Experimental Social Psychology, 3,* 1–24. doi:10.1016/0022-1031(67)90034-0

Jones, R. J., Woods, S. A., & Guillaume, Y. R. F. (2016). The effectiveness of workplace coaching: A meta-analysis of learning and performance outcomes from coaching. *Journal of Occupational and Organizational Psychology, 89,* 249–277. doi:10.1111/joop.12119

Joseph, D. L., & Newman, D. A. (2010). Emotional intelligence: An integrative meta-analysis and cascading model. *Journal of Applied Psychology, 95,* 54–78.

Judge, T. A., Colbert, A. E., & Ilies, R. (2004). Intelligence and leadership: A quantitative review and test of theoretical propositions. *Journal of Applied Psychology, 89,* 542–552.

Kaplan, R. E. (1996). *Forceful leadership and enabling leadership: You can do both.* Greensboro, NC: Center for Creative Leadership.

Karasek, R. (1990). Lower health risk with increased job control among white collar workers. *Journal of Organizational Behaviour, 11*, 171–185.

Kerasidou, A., & Horn, R. (2016). Making space for empathy: Supporting doctors in the emotional labour of clinical care. *Biomedical Central Medical Ethics, 17*, 8. doi:10.1186/s12910-016-0091-7

Kerr, R., Garvin, J., & Heaton, N. (2006). Emotional intelligence and leadership effectiveness. *Leadership and Organization Development Journal, 27*, 265–279.

König, A. S., Graf-Vlachy, L., Bundy, J. N., & Little, L. (2018). A blessing and a curse: How CEOs' empathy affects their management of organizational crises. *Academy of Management Review*. doi: https://doi.org/10.5465/amr.2017.0387

Kram, K. E., & Cherniss, C. (2001). Developing emotional competence through relationships at work. In C. Cherniss & D. Goleman (Eds.), *The emotionally intelligent workplace* (pp. 254–285). San Francisco, CA: Jossey-Bass.

Lazarus, R. (1993). Coping theory and research: Past, present, and future. *Psychosomatic Medicine, 55*, 234–247.

Lazarus, R. S., & Folkman, S. (1984). *Stress, appraisal, and coping.* New York, NY: Springer.

Leonhardt, D. (2017, April 18). Why you'd benefit from a "Shultz Hour." *New York Times*, p. A19.

Levine, M. (2007). Pollyanna and the Glad Game: A potential contribution to positive psychology. *Journal of Positive Psychology, 2*, 219–227.

Levitin, D. J. (2014, August 10). Hit the reset button in your brain. *New York Times*, p. SR5.

Lindebaum, D., & Cassell, C. (2012). A contradiction in terms? Making sense of emotional intelligence in a construction management environment. *British Journal of Management, 23*, 65–79.

Lindebaum, D., Jordan, P. J., & Morris, L. (2015). Symmetrical and asymmetrical outcomes of leader anger expression: A qualitative study of army personnel. *Human Relations, 69*, 1–24. doi:10.1177/0018726715593350

Mackie, D., Asuncion, A., & Rosselli, F. (1992). The impact of positive affect on persuasion processes. In M. S. Clark (Ed.), *Emotion and social behavior: Review of personality and social psychology* (Vol. 14, pp. 247–270). Thousand Oaks, CA: Sage.

Mann, L. (1992). Stress, affect and risk taking. In J. F. Yates (Ed.), *Risk-taking behaviour* (pp. 201–230). Oxford, England: Wiley.

Mayer, J. D., & Salovey, P. (1997). What is emotional intelligence? In P. Salovey & D. J. Sluyter (Eds.), *Emotional development and emotional intelligence* (pp. 3–34). New York, NY: Basic Books.

Mayer, J. D., Salovey, P., & Caruso, D. R. (2000). Models of emotional intelligence. In R. J. Sternberg (Ed.), *Handbook of intelligence* (2nd ed., pp. 396–420). New York, NY: Cambridge University Press.

Mayer, J. D., Salovey, P., Caruso, D. R., & Cherkasskiy, L. (2011). Emotional intelligence. In R. J. Sternberg & S. B. Kaufman (Eds.), *The Cambridge handbook of intelligence.* (pp. 528–549). New York: Cambridge University Press.

McCall, M. W., Jr. (2013). An interview with Morgan McCall. *People & Strategy, 36*(3).

McCall, M. W., Jr., Lombardo, M. M., & Morrison, A. M. (1988). *The lessons of experience: How successful executives develop on the job.* Lexington, MA: Lexington Books.

McClelland, D. C. (1998). Identifying competencies with behavioral-event interviews. *Psychological Science, 9*, 331–339.

McGregor, D. (1960). *The human side of enterprise.* New York, NY: McGraw-Hill.

Miao, C., Humphrey, R. H., & Qian, S. (2016). Leader emotional intelligence and subordinate job satisfaction: A meta-analysis of main, mediator, and moderator effects. *Personality and Individual Differences, 102,* 13–24. doi:http://dx.doi.org/10.1016/j.paid.2016.06.056

Miller, C. C. (2011, January 22). New stage, new skills: A creator prepares to take the reins at Google. *New York Times,* pp. B1, B4.

Miller, J. R. (2010, February 15). George Washington's Tear-Jerker. *New York Times,* A21.

Mortimer, J. T., & Lorence, J. (1979). Work experience and occupational value socialization: A longitudinal study. *American Journal of Sociology, 84,* 1361–1385.

Moskowitz, J. T., Hult, J. R., Duncan, L. G., Cohn, M. A., Maurer, S., Bussolari, C., & Acree, M. (2011). A positive affect intervention for people experiencing health-related stress: Development and non-randomized pilot test. *Journal of Health Psychology, 17,* 676–692. doi:10.1177/1359105311425275

Motowidlo, S. J., Carter, G. W., Dunnette, M. D., Tippins, N., Werner, S., Burnett, J. R., & Vaughan, M. J. (1992). Studies of the structured behavioral interview. *Journal of Applied Psychology, 77,* 571–587.

Murphy, S. E. (2002). Leader self-regulation: The role of self-efficacy and multiple intelligences. In R. E. Riggio, S. E. Murphy, & F. J. Pirozzolo (Eds.), *Multiple intelligences and leadership* (pp. 163–186). Mahwah, NJ: Erlbaum.

Murphy, W., & Kram, K. E. (2014). *Strategic relationships at work: Creating your circle of mentors, sponsors, and peers for success in business and life.* New York, NY: McGraw-Hill.

Nielsen, K., Randall, R., Yarker, J., & Brenner, S. O. (2008). The effects of transformational leadership on followers' perceived work characteristics and psychological well-being: A longitudinal study. *Work and Stress, 22,* 16–32.

Norman, S. M., Avolio, B. J., & Luthans, F. (2010). The impact of positivity and transparency on trust in leaders and their perceived effectiveness. *Leadership Quarterly, 21,* 350–364. doi:10.1016/j.leaqua.2010.03.002

Orenstein, R. L. (2007). *Multidimensional executive coaching.* New York, NY: Springer.

Palmer, B. R., Stough, C., Hamer, R., & Gignac, G. E. (2009). Genos Emotional Intelligence Inventory: A measure designed specifically for workplace applications. In C. Stough, D. Saklofske, & J. D. Parker (Eds.), *Assessing emotional intelligence* (pp. 103–117). New York, NY: Springer.

Parrott, W. G. (2002). The functional utility of negative emotions. In L. F. Barrett & P. Salovey (Eds.), *The wisdom in feeling: Psychological processes in emotional intelligence* (pp. 341–359). New York, NY: Guilford Press.

Pennebaker, J., & Smith, J. M. (2016). *Opening up by writing it down.* New York, NY: Guilford Press.

Perkins, D. N. T. (2000). *Leading at the edge: Leadership lessons from the extraordinary saga of Shackleton's Antarctic expedition.* New York, NY: AMACOM.

Pescosolido, A. T. (2002). Emergent leaders as managers of group emotion. *Leadership Quarterly, 13,* 583–599.

Petrides, K. V., & Furnham, A. (2001). Trait emotional intelligence: Psychometric investigation with reference to established trait taxonomies. *European Journal of Personality, 15,* 425–448.

Plous, S. (1993). *The psychology of judgment and decision making.* New York, NY: McGraw-Hill.

Rasulzada, F., Dackert, I., & Johansson, C. R. (2003). Employee well-being in relation to organizational climate and leadership style. In *Proceedings of the Fifth European Conference of the European Academy of Occupational Health Psychology, Berlin* (pp. 220–224). Nottingham, England: Institute of Work Health and Organisations, University of Nottingham.

Rekalde, I., Landeta, J., & Albizu, E. (2015). Determining factors in the effectiveness of executive coaching as a management development tool. *Management Decision, 53,* 1677–1697. doi:10.1108/MD-12-2014-0666

Richards, J. M., & Gross, J. J. (2000). Emotion regulation and memory: The cognitive costs of keeping one's cool. *Journal of Personality and Social Psychology, 79,* 410–424.

Ronan, W. W., & Latham, G. P. (1974). The reliability and validity of the critical incident technique: A closer look. *Studies in Personnel Psychology, 6,* 53–64.

Rosete, D. (2007). *Does emotional intelligence play an important role in leadership effectiveness?* (Unpublished doctoral dissertation). University of Wollongong, Wollongong, New South Wales, Australia.

Salovey, P., & Mayer, J. (1990). Emotional intelligence. *Imagination, Cognition, and Personality, 9,* 185–211.

Sandler, I. N., Braver, S., & Gensheimer, L. (2000). Stress: Theory, research, and action. In J. Rappaport & E. Seidman (Eds.), *Handbook of community psychology* (pp. 187–214). New York, NY: Kluwer Academic/Plenum.

Sarason, S. B. (1999). *Teaching as a performing art.* New York, NY: Teachers College Press.

Schneider, K. (2014). *Transfer of learning in organizations.* Cham, Switzerland: Springer.

Scholl, A., Sassenberg, K., Scheepers, D., Ellemers, N., & de Wit, F. (2017). A matter of focus: Power-holders feel more responsible after adopting a cognitive other-focus, rather than a self-focus. *British Journal of Social Psychology, 56,* 89–102. doi:10.1111/bjso.12177

Schulman, P., Keith, D., & Seligman, M. (1993). Is optimism heritable? A study of twins. *Behavior Research and Therapy, 31,* 569–574 doi:10.1016/0005-7967(93)90108-7

Scott, B. A., Colquitt, J. A., Paddock, E. L., & Judge, T. A. (2010). A daily investigation of the role of manager empathy on employee well-being. *Organizational Behavior and Human Decision Processes, 113,* 127–140.

Seligman, M. E. P. (2002). *Authentic happiness: Using the new positive psychology to realize your potential for lasting fulfillment.* New York, NY: Free Press.

Shanker, T. (2010, August 13). Win wars? Today's general must also meet, manage, placate, politick, and do P.R. *New York Times,* p. A11.

Shapiro, D. (2016). *Negotiating the nonnegotiable.* New York, NY: Viking.

Shobitha Poulose, S. N. (2014). Work life balance: A conceptual review. *International Journal of Advances in Management and Economics, 3.* Retrieved from http://www.managementjournal.info/index.php/IJAME/article/view/324

Skakon, J., Nielsen, K., Borg, V., & Guzman, J. (2010). Are leaders' well-being, behaviours and style associated with the affective well-being of their employees? A systematic review of three decades of research. *Work & Stress, 24*, 107–139.

Smollan, R., & Parry, K. (2011). Follower perceptions of the emotional intelligence of change leaders: A qualitative study. *Leadership, 7*, 435–462.

Soojung-Kim Pang, A. (2016). *Rest: Why you get more done when you work less.* New York, NY: Basic Books.

Spencer, L. M., Jr., & Spencer, S. (1993). *Competence at work: Models for superior performance.* New York, NY: Wiley.

Sternberg, R. J. (1985). *Beyond IQ: A triarchic theory of human intelligence.* New York, NY: Cambridge University Press.

Strike, V. M., Michel, A., & Kammerlander, N. (2018). Unpacking the black box of family business advising: Insights from psychology. *Family Business Review, 31*, 80–124. doi:10.1177/0894486517735169

Subramanian, S. (2013, August 19). Google took its 20% back, but other companies are making employee side projects work for them. *Fast Company Daily Newsletter.* Retrieved from https://www.fastcompany.com/3015963/google-took-its-20-back-but-other-companies-are-making-employee-side-projects-work-for-them

Sutton, R. I. (2010). *Good boss, bad boss.* New York, NY: Business Plus.

Sy, T., Horton, C., & Riggio, R. (2018). Charismatic leadership: Eliciting and channeling follower emotions. *Leadership Quarterly, 29*, 58–69. doi:https://doi.org/10.1016/j.leaqua.2017.12.008

Thompson, H. L. (2010). *The stress effect: Why smart leaders make dumb decisions—and what to do about it.* San Francisco, CA: Jossey-Bass.

Thorndike, E. L. (1920). Intelligence and its use. *Harper's Magazine, 140*, 227–235.

Ury, W. (1991). *Getting past no: Negotiating with difficult people.* New York, NY: Bantam Books.

Van Kleef, G. A. (2014). Understanding the positive and negative effects of emotional expressions in organizations: EASI does it. *Human Relations, 67*, 1145–1164.

Vroom, V. H., & Jago, A. G. (2007). The role of the situation in leadership. *American Psychologist, 62*, 17–24.

Wiens, K. (2016). *Leading through burnout: The influence of emotional intelligence on the ability of executive level physician leaders to cope with occupational stress and burnout.* (Ed.D. Doctoral dissertation), University of Pennsylvania, Philadelphia.

Wiens, K. (2017). Break the cycle of stress and distraction by using your emotional intelligence. *Harvard Business Review*, 2–5. doi:AN: 127073575

Williams, M. J. (2014). Serving the self from the seat of power: Goals and threats predict leaders' self-interested behavior. *Journal of Management, 40*, 1365–1395. doi: https://doi.org/10.1177/0149206314525203

Zaccaro, S. J. (2002). Organizational leadership and social intelligence. In R. E. Riggio, S. E. Murphy, & F. J. Pirozzolo (Eds.), *Multiple intelligences and leadership* (pp. 29–54). Mahwah, NJ: Erlbaum.

INDEX

For the benefit of digital users, indexed terms that span two pages (e.g., 52–53) may, on occasion, appear on only one of those pages.